Classic

DOG STORIES

ALSO EDITED BY NANCY BUTLER

The Quotable Lover

Classic
DOG STORIES

EDITED AND WITH
AN INTRODUCTION *by*
NANCY BUTLER

THE LYONS PRESS
GUILFORD, CONNECTICUT
AN IMPRINT OF THE GLOBE PEQUOT PRESS

The Lyons Press is an imprint of The Globe Pequot Press.

Printed in the United States of America

10   9   8   7   6   5   4   3   2   1

Text Design by Claire Zoghb

ISBN 1-59228-457-4

Library of Congress Cataloging-in-Publication Data
is available on file.

This is for my own dogs: Sparrow, aka Rutabagozers, a difficult dog but a very good basenji, and Stacy, aka Happy Dog, a cocker-Lab mix who retrieved rocks and bowling balls.

And for all the dogs I've known personally (or heard tall tales about): Bogie the shar pei, Brady the boxer, Murphy the golden retriever, Beorn the Norwegian elkhound, Missy the collie cross, McChesney the wire-haired fox terrier, Percy the mutt, Lobo the shepherd-husky, Max the white boxer, Cleo the dachsy mutt, Ginger Jones the cocker spaniel, Gigi and Lolita the Brittany spaniels, Lucky the setter, Oona and Oliver the greyhounds, Poncho and Fabian the chihuahuas, and Sammy Jo the Pekingese.

And for Pudgie, my father's first dog, who followed my grandmother to church and thus became a key source of a long family tradition of storytelling.

Contents

CONTENTS

Introduction

"Humans were denied the speech of animals. The only common ground of communication upon which dogs and men can get together is in fiction."

—*O. Henry*

For thousands of years, dogs have served men and women . . . as protectors of the home, hunters and retrievers of game, and guardians of the herd. But perhaps the most enduring and valued role that canines have played is that of devoted human companion. Children delight in rough–housing with dogs and adults find some reflection of their own souls in the warm, bright eyes of their favorite pet. Even the gruffest master must feel some bond of kinship at the end of the day when he relaxes with his faithful hound at his feet.

Yet in many of these classic stories, which hail from a time of an earlier, almost foreign sensibility, dogs do not always get their day. It's difficult to believe when viewing the pampered pets on parade in any large city that dogs once had it so hard. They toiled daily in the service of their owners and were lucky if they were rewarded with an offhand pat or an old soup bone. And while some writers sentimentalize the strong bond between man and dog and others lampoon the love/hate relationship between hapless owners and clever canines, a number of these stories demonstrate the cavalier, if not downright cruel treatment dogs received. These crusading authors took up their pens to expose the frequent indifference to the plight of dogs so that people in general would look upon them with kindness and tolerance. They wanted every dog owner to gain a keener understanding of the friend who walks so faithfully at his or her side.

Focusing on the sometimes precarious relationship between human and dog, this collection begins with an excerpt from *Beautiful Joe*, by Marshall Saunders. This is the beloved tale of an ugly, misfit mongrel who suffers at the hands of his first owner until at last he finds a loving home. The book was written as a response to *Black Beauty*, which told a similar tale

of a horse's odyssey through life, withstanding ignorance and harsh treatment until he, too, finds his
own green pastures. *Beautiful Joe* was an attempt to
make readers aware of the casual mistreatment of
dogs, which can be seen in "Uncle Dick's Rolf" by
Georgiana M. Craik. Even though this is a story of
a dog's loyalty and uncanny prescience, Rolf's
owner strikes out at him when the dog's behavior
grows irrational. But that does not deter Rolf from
risking his own life to save Uncle Dick from the
jaws of death—literally.

O. Henry, that master of the surprise ending,
leaves us guessing at the end of "Ulysses and the
Dogman." It is difficult to be sure who is the pet—
the bulldog on the leash or the former cowhand
who walks him every night at the behest of his
wealthy, citified wife. When the husband at last
declares his independence, it is the dog, and not the
wife, who takes the brunt of his master's frustration.

In "The Baron's Wonderful Dog," a droll excerpt
from R. E. Raspe's classic, *The Surprising Adventures
of the Renowned Baron Munchausen,* a marvelous beast
exceeds her owner's expectations—and proves that
tall tales were not limited to the American West.

City life was rough on dogs in the nineteenth cen-
tury. Gangs of boys tormented them, dog catchers
rounded them up for extermination, and starvation
lurked around every dark corner. It took a plucky

dog to make his way in the urban jungle. In Stephen Crane's "A Dark-Brown Dog," one little mongrel has found a home in the city, but the tenement where he lives turns out to be more of a hell than a haven. The love of a child is not enough to prevent tragedy in the face of a parent's drunken rage. On a merrier note is O. Henry's "Memoirs of a Yellow Dog," which tells the tale of a city dog who, along with his master, longs for the freedom of the robust, country life.

One place in America where dogs flourished was the West. Whether herding, hunting, or just going along for the ride, dogs must have found the land of wide open spaces to be something of a doggy heaven. Jack London, author of *Call of the Wild* and *White Fang,* among a host of gripping and gritty dog stories, creates a poignant tale of torn loyalties in "Brown Wolf." Wolf is a dog with a past, but the young couple who try to tame him when he turns up wounded at their ranch, can have no way of knowing his origins. What is more puzzling are his constant attempts to run away—heading always to the north. It is only by sheerest coincidence that they discover the truth about their wandering dog, a painful truth that draws them into a contest that only the most loving and generous owners would agree to.

Short story author Bret Harte was known for his picaresque evocations of the denizens of the Old

West. His "A Yellow Dog" is a raffish canine who is the local miscreant in the mining camp called Rattlers Ridge. The locals simultaneously revile him and brag about his exploits. When a "good woman" visits the camp, she wins over the entire male population, but are her sweet words enough to turn that "yaller" dog from his wicked ways?

From the prolific pen of Ernest Thompson Seton, who numbered among his achievements author, naturalist, illustrator, and co-founder of the Boy Scouts of America, comes the tale of "Bingo," a dog of the West that has just a little too much adventure in his soul. Run-ins with wolves and poisoned horse carcasses don't deter Bingo from roaming free on the Plains. Though he and his master share an uneasy partnership, in the end he is a dog who comes through for those he loves.

Even in the most spoiled lapdog, at the moment of household threat or peril to its owner, there shines the shrewd, capable eyes of the wolf. Dogs owe a great deal to their feral ancestors—the pack mentality that made them seek out and cooperate with men, the need for an alpha leader that makes them obey their human masters, and the potential for great depths of affection, which wolves regularly lavish on their mates and pups.

H. H. Munro was better known as short story master Saki. He possessed an amused and slightly skewed view of his fellow man and was the literary purveyor of casual social atrocities. In "The She-Wolf," which might easily be called "A Lady in Wolf's Clothing," a pompous gentleman arouses the ire of his hostess with his constant blustering on matters metaphysical. When she coaxes a sympathetic guest at her houseparty to take part in a cunning plan to bring the braggart down a peg or two, a sugar-loving wolf named Louisa neatly steps in to complete the hoax.

"Tito: The Story of the Coyote That Learned How," is another offering from wildlife fiction mainstay Ernest Thompson Seton. While still a pup, Tito is captured by a rancher, and quickly learns the ways of men. When her wild nature stirs, she returns to the life she was born for—taking a mate and bearing her own litter of pups. But trouble lurks nearby as an old adversary stalks Tito's new family, and she must use all the wiles she acquired in captivity to best her enemy. This is a truly tender evocation of a wild parent and her offspring, quite unusual for the time it was written. Without anthropomorphizing Tito, the author makes her spring to life, as finely drawn and compelling as any human protagonist.

Whether it is leading the blind, aiding the disabled as a companion animal, sniffing out victims of an earthquake, escorting a patrolman on his nightly beat, or guarding the perimeter of an army camp, dogs excel in service-oriented jobs. Their intelligence, fortitude, and ability to think through dangerous situations are unquestioned, and their noble inclination is to always put their human companions first. "A Fire-fighter's Dog," is Arthur Quiller-Couch's homage to a singular dog that was fascinated by fires . . . nearly as much as the men who fought them. He left a legacy of bravery in the London fire brigade he served, and even after death came to the rescue of a fireman's widow and family.

Lucia Chamberlain's "Scrap" is not your average stray dog—he badly wants to be part of a military company. He finds a potential advocate in salty Sergeant Muldoon, but is still unable to win over the starchy colonel, who declares that all uncollared camp dogs must be shot. It takes the combined efforts of the whole regiment to show that Scrap has "won his stripes." Another story of a military dog is "Carlo, A Soldiers' Dog," a memoir by Rush C. Hawkins that follows the illustrious career of a real dog who served with the Ninth New York Volunteers during the Civil War. Although wounded in battle, Carlo, in true soldiers' tradition, never abandoned his regiment and went on to an honorable retirement.

Albert Payson Terhune, who made *Lad: A Dog* into a legend of animal fiction and elevated collies to the rank of canine demigods, addresses the harsh realities of dogs going to war in "Bruce." This excerpt deals with a group of soldiers in the trenches of World War I who have befriended a courier dog. When Bruce's friends go reconnoitering and find themselves trapped in a pea soup–heavy fog behind German lines, he must use all his canny instincts to bring them back to safety.

There is a saying that "nobody loves their dogs like the English." That goes likewise for the Irish, Scots, and Welsh, nationalities that have given us some of the most beloved dog breeds. The British take dogs on trains and buses and into shops and museums. Small wonder that this animal-loving nation established a society to prevent cruelty to animals before they created a similar agency to protect working children. British humorist Jerome K. Jerome clearly loves and understands dogs, but in his epic romp, *Thee Men in a Boat (To Say Nothing of the Dog)*, he gives us a waggish fox terrier named Montmorency, who is surely the wickedest dog in the whole kingdom. Focusing on Montmorency's travails as his owner and two friends embark on a "restorative" boating trip along the Thames, this collection of excerpts must surely whet the reader's appetite to consume the whole of Jerome's witty and wonderful story.

Fox hunting has fallen out of favor, but when E. Somerville and Martin Ross wrote their classic *Some Experiences of an Irish, R. M.,* it was still the rage for upper-class gents and their wives to mount up at the first cry of "Tally ho!" Yet all is not as it seems when the story's English narrator and his new wife try to win over their Irish neighbors by taking part in "Philippa's Fox-Hunt." The hounds are chasing after the fox, the erstwhile hero is riding (badly) after the hounds—but what on earth is Philippa doing on that bicycle? A wry, amusing story that offers a surprisingly modern take on the "unspeakable in pursuit of the inedible," as Oscar Wilde called fox hunting.

There are books read in childhood that linger long into adulthood and Alfred Ollivant's *Bob, Son of Battle* is one such story. In the rocky dales of Yorkshire, a rogue dog called the "Black Killer" is slaying the local sheep. Two men, longtime enemies, face off, each defending his dog, each secretly fearing that the Black Killer is his own beloved pet. When the reckoning occurs, however, it is the two dogs—Ould Bob, the champion sheepdog, and Red Wull, the mongrel ruffian—who sort things out in a climax that is breathtaking and heartbreaking. In the end it is clear that nothing brings enemies together like the shared love of dogs.

These are stories to laugh over, to weep over, and to shake your head over, knowing that the nature of dogs (and their humans) has not altered in all the years since these stories were first written. Exemplars of unconditional love, dogs offer companionship without complaint and loyalty without a price. As one literary dog lover declared, "If dogs don't go to heaven, I want to go where they go when I die."

Beautiful Joe

[MARSHALL SAUNDERS]

I
ONLY A CUR

My name is Beautiful Joe, and I am a brown dog of medium size. I am not called Beautiful Joe because I am a beauty. Mr. Morris, the clergyman, in whose family I have lived for the last twelve years, says that he thinks I must be called Beautiful Joe for the same reason that his grandfather, down South, called a very ugly colored slave-lad Cupid, and his mother Venus.

I do not know what he means by that, but when he says it people always look at me and smile. I know that I am not beautiful, and I know that I am not a thoroughbred. I am only a cur.

When my mistress went every year to register me and pay my tax, and the man in the office asked what breed I was, she said part fox-terrier and part bull-terrier; but he always put me down a cur. I don't think she liked having him call me a cur; still, I have heard her say that she preferred curs, for they have more character than well-bred dogs. Her father said that she liked ugly dogs for the same reason that a nobleman at the court of a certain king did—namely, that no one else would.

I am an old dog now, and am writing, or rather getting a friend to write, the story of my life. I have seen my mistress laughing and crying over a little book that she says is a story of a horse's life, and sometimes she puts the book down close to my nose to let me see the pictures.

I love my dear mistress; I can say no more than that; I love her better than any one else in the world; and I think it will please her if I write the story of a dog's life. She loves dumb animals, and it always grieves her to see them treated cruelly.

I have heard her say that if all the boys and girls in the world were to rise up and say that there should be no more cruelty to animals, they could put a stop to it. Perhaps it will help a little if I tell a story. I am fond of boys and girls, and though I have seen many cruel men and women, I have seen few cruel children. I think the more stories there are written about dumb animals, the better it will be for us.

In telling my story, I think I had better begin at the first and come right on to the end. I was born in a stable on the outskirts of a small town in Maine called Fairport. The first thing I remember was lying close to my mother and being very snug and warm. The next thing I remember was being always hungry. I had a number of brothers and sisters—six in all—and my mother never had enough milk for us. She was always half starved herself, so she could not feed us properly.

I am very unwilling to say much about my early life, I have lived so long in a family where there is never a harsh word spoken, and where no one thinks of ill-treating anybody or anything, that it seems almost wrong even to think or speak of such a matter as hurting a poor dumb beast.

The man that owned my mother was a milkman. He kept one horse and three cows, and he had a shaky old cart that he used to put his milk cans in. I don't think there can be a worse man in the world than that milkman. It makes me shudder now to think of him. His name was Jenkins, and I am glad to think that he is getting punished now for his cruelty to poor dumb animals and to human beings. If you think it is wrong that I am glad, you must remember that I am only a dog.

The first notice that he took of me when I was a little puppy, just able to stagger about, was to give me a kick that sent me into a corner of the stable. He used to beat and starve my mother. I have seen him use his heavy whip to punish her till her body was covered with blood. When I got older I asked her why she did not run away. She said she did not wish to; but I soon found out that the reason she did not run away, was because she loved Jenkins. Cruel and savage as he was, she yet loved him, and I believe she would have laid down her life for him.

Now that I am old, I know that there are more men in the world like Jenkins. They are not crazy, they are not drunkards; they simply seem to be possessed with a spirit of wickedness. There are well-to-do people, yes, and rich people, who will treat animals, and even little children, with such terrible cruelty, that one cannot even mention the things that they are guilty of.

One reason for Jenkins' cruelty was his idleness. After he went his rounds in the morning with his milk cans, he had nothing to do till late in the afternoon but take care of his stable and yard. If he had kept them neat, and groomed his horse, and cleaned the cows, and dug up the garden, it would have taken up all his time; but he never tidied the place at all, till his yard and stable got so littered up with things he threw down that he could not make his way about.

His house and stable stood in the middle of a large field, and they were at some distance from the road.

Passers-by could not see how untidy the place was. Occasionally, a man came to look at the premises, and see that they were in good order, but Jenkins always knew when to expect him, and had things cleaned up a little.

I used to wish that some of the people that took milk from him would come and look at his cows. In the spring and summer he drove them out to pasture, but during the winter they stood all the time in the dirty, dark stable, where the chinks in the wall were so big that the snow swept through almost in drifts. The ground was always muddy and wet; there was only one small window on the north side, where the sun only shone in for a short time in the afternoon.

They were very unhappy cows, but they stood patiently and never complained, though sometimes I know they must have nearly frozen in the bitter winds that blew through the stable on winter nights. They were lean and poor, and were never in good health. Besides being cold they were fed on very poor food.

Jenkins used to come home nearly every afternoon with a great tub in the back of his cart that was full of what he called "peelings." It was kitchen stuff that he asked the cooks at the different houses where he delivered milk, to save for him. They threw rotten vegetables, fruit parings, and scraps from the table into a tub, and gave them to him at the end of a few days. A sour, nasty mess it always was, and not fit to give any creature.

Sometimes, when he had not many "peelings," he would go to town and get a load of decayed vegetables, that grocers were glad to have him take off their hands.

This food, together with poor hay, made the cows give very poor milk, and Jenkins used to put some white powder in it, to give it "body," as he said.

Once a very sad thing happened about the milk, that no one knew about but Jenkins and his wife. She was a poor, unhappy creature, very frightened of her husband, and not daring to speak much to him. She was not a clean woman, and I never saw a worse-looking house than she kept.

She used to do very queer things, that I know now no housekeeper should do. I have seen her catch up the broom to pound potatoes in the pot. She pounded with the handle, and the broom would fly up and down in the air, dropping dust into the pot where the potatoes were. Her pan of soft-mixed bread she often left uncovered in the kitchen, and sometimes the hens walked in and sat in it.

The children used to play in mud puddles about the door. It was the youngest of them that sickened with some kind of fever early in the spring, before Jenkins began driving the cows out to pasture. The child was very ill, and Mrs. Jenkins wanted to send for a doctor, but her husband would not let her. They made a bed in the kitchen, close to the stove, and Mrs. Jenkins nursed the child as best she could. She did all her work near by, and I saw her several times wiping the child's face with the cloth that she used for washing her milk pans.

Nobody knew outside the family that the little girl was ill. Jenkins had such a bad name, that none of the neighbors would visit them. By-and-by the child got well, and a week or two later Jenkins came home with quite a frightened face, and told his wife that the husband of one of his customers was very ill with typhoid fever.

After a time the gentleman died, and the cook told Jenkins that the doctor wondered how he could have taken the fever, for there was not a case in town.

There was a widow left with three orphans, and they never knew that they had to blame a dirty, careless milkman for taking a kind husband and father from them. . . .

II
THE CRUEL MILKMAN

I have said that Jenkins spent most of his days in idleness. He had to start out very early in the morning, in order to supply his customers with milk for breakfast. Oh, how ugly he used to be, when he came into the stable on cold winter mornings, before the sun was up.

He would hang his lantern on a hook, and get his milking stool, and if the cows did not step aside just to suit him, he would seize a broom or fork, and beat them cruelly.

My mother and I slept on a heap of straw in the corner of the stable, and when she heard his step in the morning she always roused me, so that we could run out-doors as soon as he opened the stable door. He always aimed a kick at us as we passed, but my mother taught me how to dodge him.

After he finished milking, he took the pails of milk up to the house for Mrs. Jenkins to strain and put in the cans, and he came back and harnessed his horse to the cart. His horse was called Toby, and a poor, miserable, broken-down creature he was. He was weak in the knees, and weak in the back, and weak all over, and Jenkins had to beat him all the time, to make him go. He had been a cab horse, and his mouth had been jerked, and twisted, and sawed at, till one would think there could be no feeling left in it; still I have seen him wince and curl up his lip when Jenkins thrust in the frosty bit on a winter's morning.

Poor old Toby! I used to lie on my straw sometimes and wonder he did not cry out with pain. Cold and half starved he always was in the winter time, and often with raw sores on his body that Jenkins would try to hide by putting bits of cloth under the harness. But Toby never murmured, and he never tried to kick and bite, and he minded the least word from Jenkins, and if he swore at him, Toby would start back, or step up quickly, he was so anxious to please him.

After Jenkins put him in the cart, and took in the cans, he set out on his rounds. My mother, whose name was Jess, always went with him. I used to ask her why she followed such a brute of a man, and she would hang her head, and say that sometimes she got a bone from the different houses they stopped at. But that was not the whole reason. She liked Jenkins so much, that she wanted to be with him.

I had not her sweet and patient disposition, and I would not go with her. I watched her out of sight, and then ran up to the house to see if Mrs. Jenkins had any scraps for me. I nearly always got something, for she pitied me, and often gave me a kind word or look with the bits of food that she threw to me.

When Jenkins came home, I often coaxed mother to run about and see some of the neighbors' dogs with me. But she never would, and I would not leave her. So, from morning to night we had to sneak about, keeping out of Jenkins' way as much as we could, and yet trying to keep him in sight. He always sauntered about with a pipe in his mouth, and his hands in his pockets, growling first at his wife and children, and then at his dumb creatures.

I have not told what became of my brothers and sisters. One rainy day, when we were eight weeks old, Jenkins, followed by two or three of his ragged, dirty children, came into the stable and looked at us. Then he began to swear because we were so ugly, and said if we had been good-looking, he might have sold some of us. Mother watched him anxiously, and fearing some danger to her puppies, ran and jumped in the middle of us, and looked pleadingly up at him.

It only made him swear the more. He took one pup after another, and right there, before his children and my poor distracted mother, put an end to their lives. Some of them he seized by the legs and knocked against the stalls, till their brains were dashed out, others he killed with a fork. It was very terrible. My mother ran up and down the stable, screaming with pain, and I lay weak and trembling, and expecting every instant that my turn would come next. I don't know why he spared me. I was the only one left.

His children cried, and he sent them out of the stable and went out himself. Mother picked up all the puppies and brought them to our nest in the straw and licked them, and tried to bring them back to life; but it was of no use; they were quite dead. We had them in our corner of the stable for some days, till Jenkins discovered them, and swearing horribly at us, he took his stable fork and threw them out in the yard, and put some earth over them.

My mother never seemed the same after this. She was weak and miserable, and though she was only four years old, she seemed like an old dog. This was on account of the poor food she had been fed on. She could not run after Jenkins, and she lay on our heap of straw, only turning over with her nose the scraps of food I brought her to eat. One day she licked me gently, wagged her tail, and died.

As I sat by her, feeling lonely and miserable, Jenkins came into the stable. I could not bear to look at him. He had killed my mother. There she lay, a little, gaunt, scarred creature, starved and worried to death by him. Her mouth was half open, her eyes were staring. She would never again look kindly at me, or curl up to me at night to keep me warm. Oh, how I hated her murderer! But I sat quietly, even when he went up and turned her over with his foot to see if she was really dead. I think he was a little sorry, for he turned scornfully toward me and said, "She was worth two of you; why didn't you go instead?"

Still I kept quiet till he walked up to me and kicked at me. My heart was nearly broken, and I could stand no more. I flew at him and gave him a savage bite on the ankle.

"Oho," he said, "so you are going to be a fighter, are you? I'll fix you for that." His face was red and furious. He seized me by the back of the neck and carried me out to the yard where a log lay on the ground. "Bill," he called to one of his children, "bring me the hatchet."

He laid my head on the log and pressed one hand on my struggling body. I was now a year old and a full-sized dog. There was a quick, dreadful pain, and he had cut off my ear, not in the way they cut puppies' ears, but close to my head, so close that he cut off some of the skin beyond it. Then he cut off the other ear, and, turning me swiftly round, cut off my tail close to my body.

Then he let me go and stood looking at me as I rolled on the ground and yelped in agony. He was in such a passion that he did not think that people passing by on the road might hear me. . . .

III
MY KIND DELIVERER
AND MISS LAURA

There was a young man going by on a bicycle. He heard my screams and springing off his bicycle, came hurrying up the path, and stood among us before Jenkins caught sight of him.

In the midst of my pain, I heard him in say fiercely "What have you been doing to that dog?"

"I've been cuttin' his ears for fightin', my young gentleman," said Jenkins. "There is no law to prevent that, is there?"

"And there is no law to prevent my giving you a beating," said the young man, angrily. In a trice he had seized Jenkins by the throat, and was pounding him with all his might. Mrs. Jenkins came and stood at the house door, crying, but making no effort to help her husband.

"Bring me a towel," the young man cried to her, after he had stretched Jenkins, bruised and frightened, on the ground. She snatched off her apron, and ran down with it, and the young man wrapped me in it, and taking me carefully in his arms, walked down the path to the gate. There were some little boys standing there, watching him, their mouths wide open with astonishment. "Sonny," he said to the largest of them, "if you will come behind and carry this dog, I will give you a quarter."

The boy took me, and we set out. I was all smothered up in a cloth, and moaning with pain, but still I looked out occasionally to see which way we were going. We took the road to the town and stopped in front of a house on Washington Street. The young man leaned his bicycle up against the house, took a quarter from his pocket and put it in the boy's hand, and lifting me gently in his arms, went up a lane leading to the back of the house.

There was a small stable there. He went into it, put me down on the floor and uncovered my body. Some boys were playing about the stable, and I heard them say, in horrified tones, "Oh, Cousin Harry, what is the matter with that dog?"

"Hush," he said. "Don't make a fuss. You, Jack, go down to the kitchen and ask Mary for a basin of warm water and a sponge, and don't let your mother or Laura hear you."

A few minutes later, the young man had bathed my bleeding ears and tail, and had rubbed something on them that was cool and pleasant, and had bandaged them firmly with strips of cotton. I felt much better and was able to look about me.

I was in a small stable, that was evidently not used for a stable, but more for a play-room. There were various kinds of toys scattered about and a swing and bar, such as boys love to twist about on, in two different corners. In a box against the wall was a guinea pig, looking at me in an interested way. This guinea pig's name was Jeff, and he and I became good friends. A long-haired French rabbit was hopping about, and a tame white rat was perched on the shoulder of one of the boys, and kept his foothold there, no matter how suddenly the boy moved. There were so many boys, and the stable was so small, that I suppose he was afraid he would get stepped on if he went on the floor. He stared hard at me with his little, red eyes, and never even glanced at a queer-looking, gray cat that was watching me, too, from her bed in the back of the vacant horse stall.

Out in the sunny yard, some pigeons were pecking at grain, and a spaniel lay asleep in a corner.

I had never seen anything like this before, and my wonder at it almost drove the pain away. Mother and I always chased rats and birds, and once we killed a kitten. While I was puzzling over it, one of the boys cried out, "Here is Laura!"

"Take that rag out of the way," said Mr. Harry, kicking aside the old apron I had been wrapped in, and that was stained with my blood. One of the boys stuffed it into a barrel, and then they all looked toward the house.

A young girl, holding up one hand to shade her eyes from the sun, was coming up the walk that led from the house to the stable. I thought then that I never had seen such a beautiful girl, and I think so still. She was tall and slender, and had lovely brown eyes and brown hair, and a sweet smile, and just to look at her was enough to make one love her. I stood in the stable door, staring at her with all my might.

"Why, what a funny dog," she said, and stopped short to looked at me. Up to this, I had not thought what a queer-looking sight I must be. Now I twisted round my head, saw the white bandage on my tail, and knowing I was not a fit spectacle for a pretty young lady like that, I slunk into a corner.

"Poor doggie, have I hurt your feelings?" she said, and with a sweet smile at the boys, she passed by them and came up to the guinea pig's box, behind which I had taken refuge. "What is the matter with your head, good dog?" she said, curiously, as she stooped over me.

"He has a cold in it," said one of the boys with a laugh; "so we put a nightcap on." She drew back, and turned very pale. "Cousin Harry, there are drops of blood on this cotton. Who has hurt this dog?"

"Dear Laura," and the young man coming up, laid his hand on her shoulder, "he got hurt, and I have been bandaging him."

"Who hurt him?"

"I had rather not tell you."

"But I wish to know." Her voice was as gentle as ever, but she spoke so decidedly that the young man was obliged to tell her everything. All the time he was speaking, she kept touching me gently with her fingers. When he had finished his account of rescuing me from Jenkins, she said, quietly:

"You will have the man punished?"

"What is the use? That won't stop him from being cruel."

"It will put a check on his cruelty."

"I don't think it would do any good," said the young man, doggedly.

"Cousin Harry!" and the young girl stood up very straight and tall, her brown eyes flashing, and one hand pointing at me; "Will you let that pass? That animal has been wronged, it looks to you to right it. The coward who has maimed it for life should be punished. A child has a voice to tell its wrong—a poor, dumb creature must suffer in silence; in bitter, bitter silence. And," eagerly, as the young man tried to interrupt her, "you are doing the man himself an injustice. If he is bad enough to ill-treat his dog, he will ill-treat his wife and children. If he is checked and punished now for his cruelty, he may reform. And even if his wicked heart is not changed, he will be obliged to treat them with outward kindness, through fear of punishment."

The young man looked convinced, and almost as ashamed as if he had been the one to crop my ears. "What do you want me to do?" he said, slowly, and looking sheepishly at the boys who were staring open-mouthed at him and the young girl.

The girl pulled a little watch from her belt. "I want you to report that man immediately. It is now five o'clock. I will go down to the police station with you, if you like."

"Very well," he said, his face brightening, and together they went off to the house.

IV
THE MORRIS BOYS
ADD TO MY NAME

The boys watched them out of sight, then one of them, whose name I afterward learned was Jack, and who came next to Miss Laura in age, gave a low whistle and said, "Doesn't the old lady come out strong when any one or anything gets abused? I'll never forget the day she found me setting Jim on that black cat of the Wilsons. She scolded me, and then she cried, till I didn't know where to look. Plague on it, how was I going to know he'd kill the old cat? I only wanted to drive it out of the yard. Come on, let's look at the dog."

They all came and bent over me, as I lay on the floor in my corner. I wasn't much used to boys, and I didn't know how they would treat me. But I soon found by the way they handled me and talked to me, that they knew a good deal about dogs, and were accustomed to treat them kindly. It seemed very strange to have them pat me, and call me "good dog." No one had ever said that to me before today.

"He's not much of a beauty, is he?" said one of the boys, whom they called Tom.

"Not by a long shot," said Jack Morris, with a laugh. "Not any nearer the beauty mark than yourself, Tom."

Tom flew at him, and they had a scuffle. The other boys paid no attention to them, but went on looking at me. One of them, a little boy with eyes like Miss Laura's, said, "What did Cousin Harry say the dog's name was?"

"Joe," answered another boy. "The little chap that carried him home told him."

"We might call him 'Ugly Joe' then," said a lad with a round, fat face, and laughing eyes. I wondered very much who this boy was, and, later on, I found out that he was another of Miss Laura's brothers, and his name was Ned. There seemed to be no end to the Morris boys.

"I don't think Laura would like that," said Jack Morris, suddenly coming up behind him. He was very hot, and was breathing fast, but his manner was as cool as if he had never left the group about me. He had beaten Tom, who was sitting on a box, ruefully surveying a hole in his jacket. "You see," he went on, gaspingly, "if you call him 'Ugly Joe,' her ladyship will say that you are wounding the dear dog's feelings. 'Beautiful Joe,' would be more to her liking."

A shout went up from the boys. I didn't wonder that they laughed. Plain-looking I naturally was; but I must have been hideous in those bandages.

"'Beautiful Joe,' then let it be!" they cried. "Let us go and tell mother, and ask her to give us something for our beauty to eat."

They all trooped out of the stable, and I was very sorry, for when they were with me, I did not mind so much the tingling in my ears, and the terrible pain in my back. They soon brought me some nice food, but I could not touch it; so they went away to their play, and I lay in the box they put me in, trembling with pain, and wishing that the pretty young lady was there, to stroke me with her gentle fingers.

By-and-by it got dark. The boys finished their play, and went into the house, and I saw lights twinkling in the windows. I felt lonely and miserable in this strange place. I would not have gone back to Jenkins' for the world, still it was the only home I had known, and though I felt that I should be happy here, I had not yet gotten used to the change. Then the pain all through my body was dreadful. My head seemed to be on fire, and there were sharp, darting pains up and down my backbone. I did not dare to howl, lest I should make the big dog, Jim, angry. He was sleeping in a kennel, out in the yard.

The stable was very quiet. Up in the loft above, some rabbits that I had heard running about had now gone to sleep. The guinea pig was nestling in the corner of his box, and the cat and the tame rat had scampered into the house long ago.

At last I could bear the pain no longer, I sat up in my box and looked about me. I felt as if I was going to die, and, though I was very weak, there was something inside me that made me feel as if I wanted to crawl away somewhere out of sight. I slunk out into the yard, and along the stable wall, where there was a thick clump of raspberry bushes. I crept in among them and lay down in the damp earth. I tried to scratch off my bandages, but they were fastened on too firmly, and I could not do it. I thought about my poor mother, and wished she was here to lick my sore ears. Though she was so unhappy herself, she never wanted to see me suffer. If I had not disobeyed her, I would not now be suffering so much pain. She had told me again and again not to snap at Jenkins, for it made him worse.

In the midst of my trouble I heard a soft voice calling, "Joe! Joe!" It was Miss Laura's voice, but I felt as if there were weights on my paws, and I could not go to her.

"Joe! Joe!" she said, again. She was going up the walk to the stable, holding up a lighted lamp in her hand. She had on a white dress, and I watched her till she disappeared in the stable. She did not stay long in there. She came out and stood on the gravel. "Joe, Joe, Beautiful Joe, where are you? You are hiding somewhere, but I shall find you." Then she came right to the spot where I was. "Poor doggie," she said, stooping down and patting me. "Are you very miserable, and did you crawl away to die? I have had dogs do that before, but I am not going to let you die, Joe." And she set her lamp on the ground, and took me in her arms.

I was very thin then, not nearly so fat as I am now, still I was quite an armful for her. But she did not seem to find me heavy. She took me right into the house, through the back door, and down a long flight of steps, across a hall, and into a snug kitchen.

"For the land sakes, Miss Laura," said a woman who was bending over a stove, "what have you got there?"

"A poor sick dog, Mary," said Miss Laura, seating herself on a chair. "Will you please warm a little milk for him? And have you a box or a basket down here that he can lie in?"

"I guess so," said the woman; "but he's awful dirty; you're not going to let him sleep in the house, are you?"

"Only for to-night. He is very ill. A dreadful thing happened to him, Mary." And Miss Laura went on to tell her how my ears had been cut off.

"Oh, that's the dog the boys were talking about," said the woman. "Poor creature, he's welcome to all I can do for him." She opened a closet door, and brought out a box, and folded a piece of blanket for me to lie on. Then she heated some milk in a saucepan, and poured it in a saucer, and watched me while Miss Laura went upstairs to get a little bottle of something that would make me sleep. They poured a few drops of this medicine into the milk and offered it to me.

I lapped a little, but I could not finish it, even though Miss Laura coaxed me very gently to do so. She dipped her finger in the milk and held it out to me, and though I did not want it, I could not be ungrateful enough to refuse to lick her finger as often as she offered it to me. After the milk was gone, Mary lifted up my box, and carried me into the washroom that was off the kitchen.

I soon fell sound asleep, and could not rouse myself through the night, even though I both smelled and heard some one coming near me several times. The next morning I found out that it was Miss Laura. Whenever there was a sick animal in the house, no matter if it was only the tame rat, she would get up two or three times in the night, to see if there was anything she could do to make it more comfortable.

Uncle Dick's Rolf

[GEORGIANA M. CRAIK]

"I had been riding for five or six miles one pleasant afternoon. It was a delicious afternoon, like the afternoon of an English summer day. You always imagine it hotter out in Africa by a good deal than it is in England, don't you? Well, so it is, in a general way, a vast deal hotter; but every now and then, after the rains have fallen and the wind comes blowing from the sea, we get a day as much like one of our own best summer days as you ever felt anywhere. This afternoon was just like an English summer afternoon, with the fresh sweet breeze rustling amongst the green leaves, and the great bright sea stretching out all blue and golden, and meeting the blue sky miles and miles away.

"It wasn't very hot, but it was just hot enough to make the thought of a swim delicious; so after I had been riding leisurely along for some little time, shooting a bird or two as I went,—for I wanted some bright feathers to send home to a little cousin that I had in England,—I alighted from my horse, and, letting him loose to graze, lay down for a quarter of an hour to cool myself, and then began to make ready for my plunge.

"I was standing on a little ledge of cliff, some six or seven feet above the sea. It was high tide, and the water at my feet was about a fathom deep. 'I shall have a delightful swim,' I thought to myself, as I threw off my coat; and as just at that moment Rolf in a very excited way flung himself upon me, evidently understanding the meaning of the proceeding, and, as I thought, anxious to show his sympathy with it, I repeated the remark aloud. 'Yes, we'll have a delightful swim, you and I together,' I said. 'A grand swim, my old lad'; and I clapped his back as I spoke, and encouraged him, as I was in the habit of doing, to express his feelings without reserve. But, rather to my surprise, instead of wagging his tail, and wrinkling his nose, and performing any of his usual antics, the creature only lifted up his face and began to whine. He had lain, for the quarter of an hour while I had been resting, at the edge of the little cliff, with his head dropped over it; but whether he had been taking a sleep in that position, or had been amusing himself by watching the waves, was more than I knew. He was a capital one for sleeping even then, and generally made a point of snatching a doze at every convenient opportunity; so I had naturally troubled my head very little about him, taking it for granted that he was at his usual occupation. But, whether he had been asleep before or not, at any rate he was wide awake now, and, as it seemed to me, in a very odd humor indeed.

"'What's the matter, old fellow?' I said to him, when he set up this dismal howl. 'Don't you want to have a swim? Well, you needn't unless you like, only *I* mean to have one; so down with you, and let me get my clothes off.' But, instead of getting down, the creature began to conduct himself in the most incomprehensible way, first seizing me by the trousers with his teeth and pulling me to the edge of the rock, as if he wanted me to plunge in dressed as I was; then catching me again and dragging me back, much as though I was a big rat that he was trying to worry; and this pantomime, I declare, he went through three separate times, barking and whining all the while, till I began to think he was going out of his mind.

"Well, God forgive me! but at last I got into a passion with the beast. I couldn't conceive what he meant. For two or three minutes I tried to pacify him, and as long as I took no more steps to get my clothes off he was willing to be pacified; but the instant I fell to undressing myself again he was on me once more, pulling me this way and that, hanging on my arms, slobbering over me, howling with his mouth up in the air. And so at last I lost my temper, and I snatched up my gun and struck him with the butt-end of it. My poor Rolf!" said Uncle Dick, all at once, with a falter in his voice; and he stopped abruptly, and stooped down and laid his hand on the great black head.

"He was quieter after I had struck him," said Uncle Dick, after a little pause. "For a few moments he lay quite still at my feet, and I had begun to think that his crazy fit was over, and that he was going to give me no more trouble, when all at once, just as I had got ready to jump into the water, the creature sprang to his feet and flung himself upon me again. He threw himself with all his might upon my breast and drove me backwards, howling so wildly that many a time since, boys, I have thought I must have been no better than a blind, perverse fool, not to have guessed what the trouble was; but the fact is, I was a conceited young fellow (as most young fellows are), and because I imagined the poor beast was trying for some reason of his own to get his own way, I thought it was my business to teach him that he was not to get his own way, but that I was to get mine; and so I beat him down somehow,—I don't like to think of it now; I struck him again three or four times with the end of my gun, till at last I got myself freed from him.

"He gave a cry when he fell back. I call it a cry, for it was more like something human than a dog's howl,—something so wild and pathetic that, angry as I was, it startled me, and I almost think, if time enough had been given me, I would have made some last attempt then to understand what the creature meant; but I had no time after that. I was standing a few feet in from the water, and as soon as I had shaken him off he went to the edge of the bit of cliff, and stood there for a moment till I came up to him, and then—just as in another second I should have jumped into the sea—my brave dog, my noble dog, gave one last whine and one look into my face, and took the leap before me. And then, boys, in another instant I saw what he had meant. He had scarcely touched the water when I saw a crocodile slip like lightning from a sunny ledge of the cliff, and grip him by the hinder legs.

"You know that I had my gun close at hand, and in the whole course of my life I never was so glad to have my gun beside me. It was loaded, too, and a revolver. I caught it up, and fired into the water. I fired three times, and two of the shots went into the brute's head. One missed him, and the first seemed not to harm him much, but the third hit him in some vital place, I hope,—some sensitive place, at any rate, for the hideous jaws started wide. Then, with my gun in my hand still, I began with all my might to shout out, 'Rolf!' I couldn't leave my post, for the brute, though he had let Rolf go, and had dived for a moment, might make another spring, and I didn't dare to take my eyes off the spot where he had gone down; but I called to my wounded beast with all my might, and when he had struggled through the water and gained a moment's hold of the rock, I jumped down and caught him, and some-how—I don't know how—half carried and half dragged him up the little bit of steep ascent, till we were safe on the top,—on the dry land again. And then upon my word, I don't know what I did next, only I think, as I looked at my darling's poor crushed limbs, with the blood oozing from them, and heard his choking gasps for breath—I—I forgot for a moment or two that I was a man at all, and burst out crying like a child.

"Boys, you don't know what it is to feel that a liv-ing creature has tried to give up his life for you, even though the creature is only a soulless dog. Do you think I had another friend in the world who would have done what Rolf had done for me? If I had, I did not know it. And then when I thought that it was while he had been trying to save my life that I had taken up my gun and struck him! There are some things, my lads, that a man does without meaning any harm by them, which yet, when he sees them by the light of after events, he can never bear to look back upon without a sort of agony; and those blows I gave to Rolf are of that sort. *He* forgave them,—my noble dog; but I have never forgiven myself for them to this hour. When I saw him lying before me, with his blood trickling out upon the sand, I think I would have given my right hand to save his life. And well I might, too, for he had done ten times more than that to save mine.

"He licked the tears off my cheeks, my poor old fellow; I remember that. We looked a strange pair, I dare say, as we lay on the ground together, with our heads side by side. It's a noble old head still, isn't it, boys? (I don't mean mine, but this big one down here. All right, Rolf! We're only talking of your beauty, my lad.) It's as grand a head as ever a dog had. I had his picture taken after I came home. I've had him painted more than once, but somehow I don't think the painters have ever seen quite into the bottom of his heart. At least, I fancy that if I were a painter I could make something better of him than any of them have done yet. Perhaps it's only a notion of mine, but, to tell the truth, I've only a dozen times or so in my life seen a painting of a grand dog that looks quite right. But I'm wandering from my story, though, indeed, my story is almost at an end.

"When I had come to my senses a little, I had to try to get my poor Rolf moved. We were a long way from any house, and the creature couldn't walk a step. I tore up my shirt, and bound his wounds as well as I could, and then I got my clothes on, and called to my horse, and in some way, as gently as I could,—though it was no easy thing to do it,—I got him and myself together upon the horse's back, and we began our ride. There was a village about four or five miles off, and I made for that. It was a long, hard jolt for a poor fellow with both his hind legs broken, but he bore it as patiently as if he had been a Christian. I never spoke to him but, panting as he was, he was ready to lick my hands and look lovingly up into my face. I've wondered since, many a time, what he could have thought about it all; and the only thing I am sure of is that he never thought much of the thing that he himself had done. That seemed, I know, all natural and simple to him; I don't believe that he has ever understood to this day what anybody wondered at in it, or made a hero of him for. For the noblest people are the people who are noble without knowing it; and the same rule, I fancy, holds good, too, for dogs.

"I got him to a resting-place at last, after a weary ride, and then I had his wounds dressed; but it was weeks before he could stand upon his feet again, and when at last he began to walk he limped, and he has gone on limping ever since. The bone of one leg was so crushed that it couldn't be set properly, and so that limb is shorter than the other three. *He* doesn't mind it much, I dare say,—I don't think he ever did,—but it has been a pathetic lameness to me, boys. It's all an old story now, you know," said Uncle Dick, abruptly, "but it's one of those things that a man doesn't forget, and that it would be a shame to him if he ever *could* forget as long as his life lasts."

Uncle Dick stooped down again as he ceased to speak, and Rolf, disturbed by the silence, raised his head to look about him. As his master had said, it was a grand old head still, though the eyes were growing dim now with age. Uncle Dick laid his hand upon it, and the bushy tail began to wag. It had wagged at the touch of that hand for many a long day.

"We've been together for fifteen years. He's getting old now," said Uncle Dick.

Ulysses and the Dogman

[O. HENRY]

Do you know the time of the dogmen? When the forefinger of twilight begins to smudge the clear-drawn lines of the Big City, there is inaugurated an hour devoted to one of the most melancholy sights of urban life.

Out from the towering flat crags and apartment peaks of the cliff-dwellers of New York steals an army of beings that were once men. Even yet they go upright upon two limbs and retain human form and speech; but you will observe that they are behind animals in progress. Each of these beings follows a dog, to which he is fastened by an artificial ligament.

These men are all victims to Circe. Not willingly do they become flunkeys to Fido, bell-boys to bull terriers, and toddlers after Towzer. Modern Circe, instead of turning them into animals, has kindly left the difference of a six-foot leash between them. Every one of these dogmen has been either cajoled, bribed, or commanded by his own particular Circe to take the dear household pet out for an airing.

By their faces and manner you can tell that the dogmen are bound in a hopeless enchantment. Never will there come even a dog-catcher Ulysses to remove the spell.

The faces of some are stonily set. They are past the commiseration, the curiosity, or the jeers of their fellow-beings. Years of matrimony, of continuous compulsory canine constitutionals, have made them callous. They unwind their beasts from lamp-posts, or the ensnared legs of profane pedestrians, with the stolidity of mandarins manipulating the strings of their kites.

Others, more recently reduced to the ranks of Rover's retinue, take their medicine sulkily and fiercely. They play the dog on the end of their line with the pleasure felt by the girl out fishing when she catches a sea-robin on her hook. They glare at you threateningly if you look at them, as if it would be their delight to let slip the dogs of war. These are half-mutinous dogmen, not quite Circe-ized, and you will do well not to kick their charges, should they sniff around your ankles.

Others of the tribe do not seem to feel so keenly. They are mostly unfresh youths, with gold caps and drooping cigarettes, who do not harmonize with their dogs. The animals they attend wear satin bows in their collars; and the young men steer them so assiduously that you are tempted to the theory that some personal advantage, contingent upon satisfactory service, waits upon the execution of their duties.

The dogs thus personally conducted are of many varieties: but they are one in fatness, in pampered, diseased vileness of temper, in insolent, snarling capriciousness of behavior. They tug at the leash fractiously, they make leisurely nasal inventory of every doorstep, railing, and post. They sit down to rest when they choose; they wheeze like the winner of a Third Avenue beefsteak-eating contest; they blunder clumsily into open cellars and coal holes; they lead the dogmen a merry dance.

These unfortunate dry nurses of dogdom, the cur cuddlers, mongrel managers, Spitz stalkers, poodle pullers, Skye scrapers, dachshund dandlers, terrier trailers and Pomeranian pushers of the cliff-dwelling Circes follow their charges meekly. The doggies neither fear nor respect them. Masters of the house these men whom they hold in leash may be, but they are not masters of them. From cozy corner to fire-escape, from divan to dumb-waiter, doggy's snarl easily drives this two-legged being who is commissioned to walk at the other end of his string during his outing.

One twilight the dogmen came forth as usual at their Circes' pleading, guerdon, or crack of the whip. One among them was a strong man, apparently of too solid virtues for this airy vocation. His expression was melancholic, his manner depressed. He was leashed to a vile, white dog, loathsomely fat, fiendishly ill-natured, gloatingly intractable toward his despised conductor.

At a corner nearest to his apartment-house the dogman turned down a side-street, hoping for fewer witnesses to his ignominy. The surfeited beast waddled before him, panting with spleen and the labor of motion.

Suddenly the dog stopped. A tall, brown, long-coated, wide-brimmed man stood like a Colossus blocking the sidewalk and declaring:

"Well, I'm a son of a gun!"

"Jim Berry!" breathed the dogman, with exclamation points in his voice.

"Sam Telfair," cried Wide-Brim again, "you ding-basted old willywalloo, give us your hoof!"

Their hands clasped in the brief, tight greeting of the West that is death to the handshake microbe.

"You old fat rascal!" continued Wide-Brim, with a wrinkled, brown smile; "it's been five years since I seen you. I been in this town a week, but you can't find nobody in such a place. Well, you dinged old married man, how are they coming?"

Something mushy and heavily soft like raised dough leaned against Jim's leg and chewed his trousers with a yeasty growl.

"Get to work," said Jim, "and explain this yard-wide hydrophobia yearling you've throwed your lasso over. Are you the pound-master of this burg? Do you call that a dog or what?"

"I need a drink," said the dogman, dejected at the reminder of his old dog of the sea. "Come on."

Hard by was a café. 'Tis ever so in the big city.

They sat at a table, and the bloated monster yelped and scrambled at the end of his leash to get at the café cat.

"Whisky," said Jim to the waiter.

"Make it two," said the dogman.

"You're fatter," said Jim, "and you look subjugated. I don't know about the East agreeing with you. All the boys asked me to hunt you up when I started. Sandy King, he went to the Klondike. Watson Burrel, he married the oldest Peters girl. I made some money buying beeves, and I bought a lot of wild land up on the Little Powder. Going to fence next fall. Bill Rawlins, he's gone to farming. You remember Bill, of course—he was courting Marcella—excuse me, Sam—I mean the lady you married, while she was teaching school at Prairie View. But you was the lucky man. How is Missis Telfair?"

"S-h-h-h!" said the dogman, signaling the waiter; "give it a name."

"Whisky," said Jim.

"Make it two," said the dogman.

"She's well," he continued, after his chaser. "She refused to live anywhere but in New York, where she came from. We live in a flat. Every evening at six I take that dog out for a walk. It's Marcella's pet. There never were two animals on earth, Jim, that hated one another like me and that dog does. His name's Lovekins. Marcella dresses for dinner while we're out. We eat tabble dote. Ever tried one of them, Jim?"

"No, I never," said Jim. "I seen the signs, but I thought they said 'table de hole.' I thought it was French for pool tables. How does it taste?"

"If you're going to be in the city for awhile we will—"

"No, sir-ee. I'm starting for home this evening on the 7:25. Like to stay longer, but I can't."

"I'll walk down to the ferry with you," said the dogman.

The dog had bound a leg each of Jim and the chair together, and had sunk into a comatose slumber. Jim stumbled and the leash was slightly wrenched. The shrieks of the awakened beast rang for a block around.

"If that's your dog," said Jim, when they were on the street again, "what's to hinder you from running that habeas corpus you've got around his neck over a limb and walking off and forgetting him?"

"I'd never dare to," said the dogman, awed at the bold proposition. "He sleeps in the bed. I sleep on a lounge. He runs howling to Marcella if I look at him. Some night, Jim, I'm going to get even with that dog. I've made up my mind to do it. I'm going to creep over with a knife and cut a hole in his mosquito bar so they can get in to him. See if I don't do it!"

"You ain't yourself, Sam Telfair. You ain't what you was once. I don't know about these cities and flats over here. With my own eyes I seen you stand off both the Tillotson boys in Prairie View with the brass faucet out of a molasses barrel. And I seen you rope and tie the wildest steer on little Powder in 39½."

"I did, didn't I?" said the other, with a temporary gleam in his eye. "But that was before I was dogmatized."

"Does Missis Telfair—" began Jim.

"Hush!" said the dogman. "Here's another café."

They lined up at the bar. The dog fell asleep at their feet.

"Whisky," said Jim.

"Make it two," said the dogman.

"I thought about you," said Jim, "when I bought that wild land. I wished you was out there to help me with the stock."

"Last Tuesday," said the dogman, "he bit me on the ankle because I asked for cream in my coffee. He always gets the cream."

"You'd like Prairie View now," said Jim. "The boys from the round-ups for fifty miles around ride in there. One corner of my pasture is in sixteen miles of the town. There's a straight forty miles of wire on one side of it."

"You pass through the kitchen to get to the bedroom," said the dogman, "and you pass through the parlor to get to the bathroom, and you back out through the dining-room to get into the bedroom so you can turn around and leave by the kitchen. And he snores and barks in his sleep, and I have to smoke in the park on account of his asthma."

"Don't Missis Telfair——" began Jim.

"Oh, shut up!" said the dogman. "What is it this time?"

"Whisky," said Jim.

"Make it two," said the dogman.

"Well, I'll be racking along down toward the ferry," said the other.

"Come on, there, you mangy, turtle-backed, snake-headed, bench-legged ton-and-a-half of soap-grease!" shouted the dogman, with a new note in his voice and a new hand on the leash. The dog scrambled after them, with an angry whine at such unusual language from his guardian.

At the foot of Twenty-third Street the dogman led the way through swinging doors.

"Last chance," said he. "Speak up."

"Whisky," said Jim.

"Make it two," said the dogman.

"I don't know," said the ranchman, "where I'll find the man I want to take charge of the Little Powder outfit. I want somebody I know something about. Finest stretch of prairie and timber you ever squinted your eye over, Sam. Now, if you was—"

"Speaking of hydrophobia," said the dogman, "the other night he chewed a piece out of my leg because I knocked a fly off of Marcella's arm. 'It ought to be cauterized,' says Marcella, and I was thinking so myself. I telephones for the doctor, and when he comes Marcella says to me: 'Help me hold the poor dear while the doctor fixes his mouth. Oh, I hope he got no virus on any of his toofies when he bit you.' Now what do you think of that?"

"Does Missis Telfair—" began Jim.

"Oh, drop it," said the dogman. "Come again!"

"Whisky," said Jim.

"Make it two," said the dogman.

They walked on to the ferry. The ranchman stepped to the ticket-window.

Suddenly the swift landing of three or four heavy kicks was heard, the air was rent by piercing canine shrieks, and a pained, outraged, lubberly, bow-legged pudding of a dog ran frenziedly up the street alone.

"Ticket to Denver," said Jim.

"Make it two," shouted the ex-dogman, reaching for his inside pocket.

The Baron's Wonderful Dog

[**R. E. RASPE**]

I had married a lady of great beauty, who, having heard of my sporting exploits, desired, a short time after our marriage, to go out with me on a shooting expedition. I went on in front to start something, and I soon saw my dog stop before several hundred coveys of partridges. I waited for my wife, who was following me with my lieutenant and a servant. I waited a long time; nobody came.

At length, very uneasy, I went back, and, when I was halfway to the place where I had left my wife, I heard lamentable groans. They seemed quite near, and yet I could see no trace of a human being. I jumped off my horse; I put my ear to the ground, and not only heard the groans distinctly rising from beneath, but my wife's voice and those of my lieutenant and servant.

I remarked at the same time, not far from the spot, the shaft of a coal-pit, and I had no doubt that my wife and her unfortunate companions had been swallowed up in it. I rode full speed to the nearest village to fetch the miners, who after great efforts succeeded in drawing the unfortunate individuals buried in the pit—which measured ninety feet—to the surface.

They first drew up the manservant; then his horse; next the lieutenant; next his horse; and at length my wife on her little palfrey. The most curious part of this affair was that, in spite of the awful depth to which they had fallen, no one was hurt, not even the horses, if we except a few slight contusions. But they had had a terrible fright, and were quite unable to pursue our intended sport.

In all this confusion I quite forgot my setter, as no doubt you also have.

The next day I was obliged to go away on duty, and did not return home for a fortnight. On my return I asked for Diana, my setter. No one knew anything about her. My servants thought she had followed me. She was certainly lost, and I never hoped to see her again! At length a bright idea occurred to me:

"She is perhaps still watching the partridges."

I hastened, full of hope and joy, to the spot, and actually there she was!—my noble Diana—on the very place where I had left her a fortnight before.

"Hi, Diana!" I cried. "Seize them!"

She instantly sprang the partridges; they rose, and I killed twenty-five at one shot. But the poor beast had scarcely strength enough to follow me, she was so thin and famished. I was obliged to carry her back to the house on my horse, where rest, feeding, and great care soon restored her to health.

I was thoroughly glad to get her back again.

Brown Wolf

[JACK LONDON]

She had delayed, because of the dew-wet grass, in order to put on her overshoes, and when she emerged from the house found her waiting husband absorbed in the wonder of a bursting almond-bud. She sent a questing glance across the tall grass and in and out among the orchard trees.

"Where's Wolf?" she asked.

"He was here a moment ago." Walt Irvine drew himself away with a jerk from the metaphysics and poetry of the organic miracle of blossom, and surveyed the landscape. "He was running a rabbit the last I saw of him."

"Wolf! Wolf! Here Wolf!" she called, as they left the clearing and took the trail that led down through the waxen-belled manzanita jungle to the county road.

Irvine thrust between his lips the little finger of each hand and lent to her efforts a shrill whistling.

She covered her ears hastily and made a wry grimace.

"My! for a poet, delicately attuned and all the rest of it, you can make unlovely noises. My eardrums are pierced. You outwhistle—"

"Orpheus."

"I was about to say a street-Arab," she concluded severely.

"Poesy does not prevent one from being practical—at least it doesn't prevent ME. Mine is no futility of genius that can't sell gems to the magazines."

He assumed a mock extravagance, and went on:

"I am no attic singer, no ballroom warbler. And why? Because I am practical. Mine is no squalor of song that cannot transmute itself, with proper exchange value, into a flower-crowned cottage, a sweet mountain-meadow, a grove of red-woods, an orchard of thirty-seven trees, one long row of blackberries and two short rows of strawberries, to say nothing of a quarter of a mile of gurgling brook. I am a beauty-merchant, a trader in song, and I pursue utility, dear Madge. I sing a song, and thanks to the magazine editors I transmute my song into a waft of the west wind sighing through our redwoods, into a murmur of waters over mossy stones that sings back to me another song than the

one I sang and yet the same song wonderfully—
er—transmuted."

"O that all your song-transmutations were as successful!" she laughed.

"Name one that wasn't."

"Those two beautiful sonnets that you transmuted
into the cow that was accounted the worst milker in
the township."

"She was beautiful—" he began,

"But she didn't give milk," Madge interrupted.

"But she *was* beautiful, now, wasn't she?" he insisted.

"And here's where beauty and utility fall out," was
her reply. "And there's the Wolf!"

From the thicket-covered hillside came a crashing
of underbrush, and then, forty feet above them, on
the edge of the sheer wall of rock, appeared a wolf's
head and shoulders. His braced fore paws dislodged a
pebble, and with sharp-pricked ears and peering eyes
he watched the fall of the pebble till it struck at their
feet. Then he transferred his gaze and with open
mouth laughed down at them.

"You Wolf, you!" and "You blessed Wolf!" the
man and woman called out to him.

The ears flattened back and down at the sound,
and the head seemed to snuggle under the caress of
an invisible hand.

They watched him scramble backward into the
thicket, then proceeded on their way. Several minutes

later, rounding a turn in the trail where the descent was less precipitous, he joined them in the midst of a miniature avalanche of pebbles and loose soil. He was not demonstrative. A pat and a rub around the ears from the man, and a more prolonged caressing from the woman, and he was away down the trail in front of them, gliding effortlessly over the ground in true wolf fashion.

In build and coat and brush he was a huge timber-wolf; but the lie was given to his wolfhood by his color and marking. There the dog unmistakably advertised itself. No wolf was ever colored like him. He was brown, deep brown, red-brown, an orgy of browns. Back and shoulders were a warm brown that paled on the sides and underneath to a yellow that was dingy because of the brown that lingered in it. The white of the throat and paws and the spots over the eyes was dirty because of the persistent and ineradicable brown, while the eyes themselves were twin topazes, golden and brown.

The man and woman loved the dog very much; perhaps this was because it had been such a task to win his love. It had been no easy matter when he first drifted in mysteriously out of nowhere to their little mountain cottage. Footsore and famished, he had killed a rabbit under their very noses and under their very windows, and then crawled away and slept by the spring at the foot of the blackberry bushes. When Walt Irvine went down to inspect the intruder, he was snarled at for his pains, and Madge likewise was snarled at when she went down to present, as a peace-offering, a large pan of bread and milk.

A most unsociable dog he proved to be, resenting all their advances, refusing to let them lay hands on him, menacing them with bared fangs and bristling hair. Nevertheless he remained, sleeping and resting by the spring, and eating the food they gave him after they set it down at a safe distance and retreated. His wretched physical condition explained why he lingered; and when he had recuperated, after several days' sojourn, he disappeared.

And this would have been the end of him, so far as Irvine and his wife were concerned, had not Irvine at that particular time been called away into the northern part of the state. Riding along on the train, near to the line between California and Oregon, he chanced to look out of the window and saw his unsociable guest sliding along the wagon road, brown and wolfish, tired yet tireless, dust-covered and soiled with two hundred miles of travel.

Now Irvine was a man of impulse, a poet. He got off the train at the next station, bought a piece of meat at a butcher shop, and captured the vagrant on the outskirts of the town. The return trip was made in the baggage car, and so Wolf came a second time to the mountain cottage. Here he was tied up for a week and made love to by the man and woman. But it was very circumspect lovemaking. Remote and alien as a traveler from another planet, he snarled down their soft-spoken love-words. He never barked. In all the time they had him he was never known to bark.

To win him became a problem. Irvine liked problems. He had a metal plate made, on which was stamped: RETURN TO WALT IRVINE, GLEN ELLEN, SONOMA COUNTY, CALIFORNIA. This was riveted to a collar and strapped about the dog's neck. Then he was turned loose, and promptly he disappeared. A day later came a telegram from Mendocino County. In twenty hours he had made over a hundred miles to the north, and was still going when captured.

He came back by Wells Fargo Express, was tied up three days, and was loosed on the fourth and lost. This time he gained southern Oregon before he was caught and returned. Always, as soon as he received his liberty, he fled away, and always he fled north. He was possessed of an obsession that drove him north. The homing instinct, Irvine called it, after he had expended the selling price of a sonnet in getting the animal back from northern Oregon.

Another time the brown wanderer succeeded in traversing half the length of California, all of Oregon, and most of Washington, before he was picked up and returned "Collect." A remarkable thing was the speed with which he traveled. Fed up and rested, as soon as he was loosed he devoted all his energy to getting over the ground. On the first day's run he was known to cover as high as a hundred and fifty miles, and after that he would average a hundred miles a day until caught. He always arrived back lean and hungry and savage, and always departed fresh and vigorous, cleaving his way northward in response to some prompting of his being that no one could understand.

But at last, after a futile year of flight, he accepted the inevitable and elected to remain at the cottage where first he had killed the rabbit and slept by the spring. Even after that, a long time elapsed before the man and woman succeeded in patting him. It was a great victory, for they alone were allowed to put hands on him. He was fastidiously exclusive, and no guest at the cottage ever succeeded in making up to him. A low growl greeted such approach; if any one had the hardihood to come nearer, the lips lifted, the naked fangs appeared, and the growl became a snarl—a snarl so terrible and malignant that it awed the stoutest of them, as it likewise awed the farmers' dogs that knew ordinary dog-snarling, but had never seen wolf-snarling before.

He was without antecedents. His history began with Walt and Madge. He had come up from the south, but never a clew did they get of the owner from whom he had evidently fled. Mrs. Johnson, their nearest neighbor and the one who supplied them with milk, proclaimed him a Klondike dog. Her brother was burrowing for frozen pay-streaks in that far country, and so she constituted herself an authority on the subject.

But they did not dispute her. There were the tips of Wolf's ears, obviously so severely frozen at some time that they would never quite heal again. Besides, he looked like the photographs of the Alaskan dogs they saw published in magazines and newspapers. They often speculated over his past, and tried to conjure up (from what they had read and heard) what his northland life had been. That the northland still drew him, they knew; for at night they sometimes heard him crying softly; and when the north wind blew and the bite of frost was in the air, a great restlessness would come upon him and he would lift a mournful lament which they knew to be the long wolf-howl. Yet he never barked. No provocation was great enough to draw from him that canine cry.

Long discussion they had, during the time of winning him, as to whose dog he was. Each claimed him, and each proclaimed loudly any expression of affection made by him. But the man had the better of it at first, chiefly because he was a man. It was patent that Wolf had had no experience with women. He did not understand women. Madge's skirts were something he never quite accepted. The swish of them was enough to set him a-bristle with suspicion, and on a windy day she could not approach him at all.

On the other hand, it was Madge who fed him; also it was she who ruled the kitchen, and it was by her favor, and her favor alone, that he was permitted to come within that sacred precinct. It was because of these things that she bade fair to overcome the handicap of her garments. Then it was that Walt put forth special effort, making it a practice to have Wolf lie at his feet while he wrote, and, between petting and talking, losing much time from his work. Walt won in the end, and his victory was most probably due to the fact that he was a man, though Madge averred that they would have had another quarter of a mile of gurgling brook, and at least two west winds sighing through their redwoods, had Wait properly devoted his energies to song-transmutation and left Wolf alone to exercise a natural taste and an unbiased judgment.

"It's about time I heard from those triolets," Walt said, after a silence of five minutes, during which they had swung steadily down the trail. "There'll be a check at the post-office, I know, and we'll transmute it into beautiful buckwheat flour, a gallon of maple syrup, and a new pair of overshoes for you."

"And into beautiful milk from Mrs. Johnson's beautiful cow," Madge added. "Tomorrow's the first of the month, you know."

Walt scowled unconsciously; then his face brightened, and he clapped his hand to his breast pocket.

"Never mind. I have here a nice beautiful new cow, the best milker in California."

"When did you write it?" she demanded eagerly. Then, reproachfully, "And you never showed it to me."

"I saved it to read to you on the way to the post office, in a spot remarkably like this one," he answered, indicating, with a wave of his hand, a dry log on which to sit.

A tiny stream flowed out of a dense fern-brake, slipped down a mossy-lipped stone, and ran across the path at their feet. From the valley arose the mellow song of meadowlarks, while about them, in and out, through sunshine and shadow, fluttered great yellow butterflies.

Up from below came another sound that broke in upon Walt reading softly from his manuscript. It was a crunching of heavy feet, punctuated now and again by the clattering of a displaced stone. As Walt finished and looked to his wife for approval, a man came into view around the turn of the trail. He was bareheaded and sweaty. With a handkerchief in one hand he mopped his face, while in the other hand he carried a new hat and a wilted starched collar which he had removed from his neck. He was a well-built man, and his muscles seemed on the point of bursting out of the painfully new and ready-made black clothes he wore.

"Warm day," Walt greeted him. Walt believed in country democracy, and never missed an opportunity to practice it.

The man paused and nodded.

"I guess I ain't used much to the warm," he vouchsafed half apologetically. "I'm more accustomed to zero weather."

"You don't find any of that in this country," Walt laughed.

"Should say not," the man answered. "An' I ain't here a-lookin' for it neither. I'm tryin' to find my sister. Mebbe you know where she lives. Her name's Johnson, Mrs. William Johnson."

"You're not her Klondike brother!" Madge cried, her eyes bright with interest, "about whom we've heard so much?"

"Yes'm, that's me," he answered modestly. "My name's Miller, Skiff Miller. I just thought I'd s'prise her."

"You are on the right track then. Only you've come by the footpath." Madge stood up to direct him, pointing up the canyon a quarter of a mile. "You see that blasted redwood? Take the little trail turning off to the right. It's the short cut to her house. You can't miss it."

"Yes'm, thank you, ma'am," he said. He made tentative efforts to go, but seemed awkwardly rooted to the spot. He was gazing at her with an open admiration of which he was quite unconscious, and which was drowning, along with him, in the rising sea of embarrassment in which he floundered.

"We'd like to hear you tell about the Klondike," Madge said. "Mayn't we come over some day while you are at your sister's? Or, better yet, won't you come over and have dinner with us?"

"Yes'm, thank you, ma'am," he mumbled mechanically. Then he caught himself up and added: "I ain't stoppin' long. I got to be pullin' north again. I go out on tonight's train. You see, I've got a mail contract with the government."

When Madge had said that it was too bad, he made another futile effort to go. But he could not take his eyes from her face. He forgot his embarrassment in his admiration, and it was her turn to flush and feel uncomfortable.

It was at this juncture, when Walt had just decided it was time for him to be saying something to relieve the strain, that Wolf, who had been away nosing through the brush, trotted wolf-like into view.

Skiff Miller's abstraction disappeared. The pretty woman before him passed out of his field of vision.

He had eyes only for the dog, and a great wonder came into his face.

"Well, I'll be damned!" he enunciated slowly and solemnly.

He sat down ponderingly on the log, leaving Madge standing. At the sound of his voice, Wolf's ears had flattened down, then his mouth had opened in a laugh. He trotted slowly up to the stranger and first smelled his hands, then licked them with his tongue.

Skiff Miller patted the dog's head, and slowly and solemnly repeated, "Well, I'll be damned!"

"Excuse me, ma'am," he said the next moment "I was just s'prised some, that was all."

"We're surprised, too," she answered lightly. "We never saw Wolf make up to a stranger before."

"Is that what you call him—Wolf?" the man asked.

Madge nodded. "But I can't understand his friendliness toward you—unless it's because you're from the Klondike. He's a Klondike dog, you know."

"Yes'm," Miller said absently. He lifted one of Wolf's fore legs and examined the foot-pads, pressing them and denting them with his thumb. "Kind of *soft*," he remarked. "He ain't been on trail for a long time."

"I say," Walt broke in, "it is remarkable the way he lets you handle him."

Skiff Miller arose, no longer awkward with admiration of Madge, and in a sharp, businesslike manner asked, "How long have you had him?"

But just then the dog, squirming and rubbing against the newcomer's legs, opened his mouth and barked. It was an explosive bark, brief and joyous, but a bark.

"That's a new one on me," Skiff Miller remarked.

Walt and Madge stared at each other. The miracle had happened. Wolf had barked.

"It's the first time he ever barked," Madge said.

"First time I ever heard him, too," Miller volunteered.

Madge smiled at him. The man was evidently a humorist.

"Of course," she said, "since you have only seen him for five minutes."

Skiff Miller looked at her sharply, seeking in her face the guile her words had led him to suspect.

"I thought you understood," he said slowly. "I thought you'd tumbled to it from his makin' up to me. He's my dog. His name ain't Wolf. It's Brown."

"Oh, Walt!" was Madge's instinctive cry to her husband.

Walt was on the defensive at once.

"How do you know he's your dog?" he demanded.

"Because he is," was the reply.

"Mere assertion," Walt said sharply.

In his slow and pondering way, Skiff Miller looked at him, then asked, with a nod of his head toward Madge:

"How d'you know she's your wife? You just say, 'Because she is,' and I'll say it's mere assertion. The dog's mine. I bred 'm an' raised 'm, an' I guess I ought to know. Look here. I'll prove it to you."

Skiff Miller turned to the dog. "Brown!" His voice rang out sharply, and at the sound the dog's ears flattened down as to a caress. "Gee!" The dog made a swinging turn to the right. "Now mush-on!" And the dog ceased his swing abruptly and started straight ahead, halting obediently at command.

"I can do it with whistles," Skiff Miller said proudly. "He was my lead dog."

"But you are not going to take him away with you?" Madge asked tremulously.

The man nodded.

"Back into that awful Klondike world of suffering?"

He nodded and added: "Oh, it ain't so bad as all that. Look at me. Pretty healthy specimen, ain't I?"

"But the dogs! The terrible hardship, the heart-breaking toil, the starvation, the frost! Oh, I've read about it and I know."

"I nearly ate him once, over on Little Fish River," Miller volunteered grimly. "If I hadn't got a moose that day was all that saved 'm."

"I'd have died first!" Madge cried.

"Things is different down here," Miller explained. "You don't have to eat dogs. You think different just about the time you're all in. You've never ben all in, so you don't know anything about it."

"That's the very point," she argued warmly. "Dogs are not eaten in California. Why not leave him here? He is happy. He'll never want for food— you know that. He'll never suffer from cold and hardship. Here all is softness and gentleness. Neither the human nor nature is savage. He will never know a whip lash again. And as for the weather—why, it never snows here."

"But it's all-fired hot in summer, beggin' your pardon," Skiff Miller laughed.

"But you do not answer," Madge continued passionately. "What have you to offer him in that northland life?"

"Grub, when I've got it, and that's most of the time," came the answer.

"And the rest of the time?"

"No grub."

"And the work?"

"Yes, plenty of work," Miller blurted out impatiently. "Work without end, an' famine, an' frost, an all the rest of the miseries—that's what he'll get when he comes with me. But he likes it. He is used to it. He knows that life. He was born to it an' brought up to it.

An' you don't know anything about it. You don't know what you're talking about. That's where the dog belongs, and that's where he'll be happiest."

"The dog doesn't go," Walt announced in a determined voice. "So there is no need of further discussion."

"What's that?" Skiff Miller demanded, his brows lowering and an obstinate flush of blood reddening his forehead.

"I said the dog doesn't go, and that settles it. I don't believe he's your dog. You may have seen him sometime. You may even sometime have driven him for his owner. But his obeying the ordinary driving commands of the Alaskan trail is no demonstration that he is yours. Any dog in Alaska would obey you as he obeyed. Besides, he is undoubtedly a valuable dog, as dogs go in Alaska, and that is sufficient explanation of your desire to get possession of him. Anyway, you've got to prove property."

Skiff Miller, cool and collected, the obstinate flush a trifle deeper on his forehead, his huge muscles bulging under the black cloth of his coat, carefully looked the poet up and down as though measuring the strength of his slenderness.

The Klondiker's face took on a contemptuous expression as he said finally, "I reckon there's nothin' in sight to prevent me takin' the dog right here an' now."

Walt's face reddened, and the striking-muscles of his arms and shoulders seemed to stiffen and grow tense. His wife fluttered apprehensively into the breach.

"Maybe Mr. Miller is right," she said. "I am afraid that he is. Wolf does seem to know him, and certainly he answers to the name of 'Brown.' He made friends with him instantly, and you know that's something he never did with anybody before. Besides, look at the way he barked. He was just bursting with joy. Joy over what? Without doubt at finding Mr. Miller."

Walt's striking-muscles relaxed, and his shoulders seemed to droop with hopelessness.

"I guess you're right, Madge," he said. "Wolf isn't Wolf, but Brown, and he must belong to Mr. Miller."

"Perhaps Mr. Miller will sell him," she suggested. "We can buy him."

Skiff Miller shook his head, no longer belligerent, but kindly, quick to be generous in response to generousness.

"I had five dogs," he said, casting about for the easiest way to temper his refusal. "He was the leader. They was the crack team of Alaska. Nothin' could touch 'em. In 1898 I refused five thousand dollars for the bunch. Dogs was high, then, anyway; but that wasn't what made the fancy price. It was the team itself. Brown was the best in the team. That winter I refused twelve hundred for 'm. I didn't sell 'm then, an' I ain't a-sellin' 'm now. Besides, I think a mighty lot of that dog. I've ben lookin' for 'm for three years. It made me fair sick when I found he'd ben stole—not the value of him, but the—well, I liked 'm like hell, that's all, beggin' your pardon. I couldn't believe my eyes when I seen 'm just now. I thought I was dreamin'. It was too good to be true. Why, I was his wet-nurse. I put 'm to bed, snug every night. His mother died, and I brought 'm up on condensed milk at two dollars a can when I couldn't afford it in my own coffee. He never knew any mother but me. He used to suck my finger regular, the darn little cuss—that finger right there!"

And Skiff Miller, too overwrought for speech, held up a forefinger for them to see.

"That very finger," he managed to articulate, as though it somehow clinched the proof of ownership and the bond of affection.

He was still gazing at his extended finger when Madge began to speak.

"But the dog," she said. "You haven't considered the dog."

Skiff Miller looked puzzled.

"Have you thought about him?" she asked.

"Don't know what you're drivin' at," was the response.

"Maybe the dog has some choice in the matter," Madge went on. "Maybe he has his likes and desires. You have not considered him. You give him no choice. It has never entered your mind that possibly he might prefer California to Alaska. You consider only what you like. You do with him as you would with a sack of potatoes or a bale of hay."

This was a new way of looking at it, and Miller was visibly impressed as he debated it in his mind. Madge took advantage of his indecision.

"If you really love him, what would be happiness to him would be your happiness also," she urged.

Skiff Miller continued to debate with himself, and Madge stole a glance of exultation to her husband, who looked back warm approval.

"What do you think?" the Klondiker suddenly demanded.

It was her turn to be puzzled. "What do you mean?" she asked.

"D'ye think he'd sooner stay in California?"

She nodded her head with positiveness. "I am sure of it."

Skiff Miller again debated with himself, though this time aloud, at the same time running his gaze in a judicial way over the mooted animal.

"He was a good worker. He's done a heap of work for me. He never loafed on me, an' he was a joe-dandy at hammerin' a raw team into shape. He's got a head on him. He can do everything but talk. He knows what you say to him. Look at 'm now. He knows we're talkin' about him."

The dog was lying at Skiff Miller's feet, head close down on paws, ears erect and listening, and eyes that were quick and eager to follow the sound of speech as it fell from the lips of first one and then the other.

"An' there's a lot of work in 'm yet. He's good for years to come. An' I do like him. I like him like hell."

Once or twice after that Skiff Miller opened his mouth and closed it again without speaking. Finally he said:

"I'll tell you what I'll do. Your remarks, ma'am, has some weight in them. The dog's worked hard, and maybe he's earned a soft berth an' has got a right to choose. Anyway, we'll leave it up to him. Whatever he says, goes. You people stay right here settin' down. I'll say good-by and walk off casual-like. If he wants to stay, he can stay. If he wants to come with me, let 'm come. I won't call 'm to come an' don't you call 'm to come back."

He looked with sudden suspicion at Madge, and added, "Only you must play fair. No persuadin' after my back is turned."

"We'll play fair," Madge began, but Skiff Miller broke in on her assurances.

"I know the ways of women," he announced. "Their hearts is soft. When their hearts is touched they're likely to stack the cards, look at the bottom of the deck, an' lie like the devil—beggin' your pardon, ma'am. I'm only discoursin' about women in general."

"I don't know how to thank you," Madge quavered.

"I don't see as you've got any call to thank me," he replied. "Brown ain't decided yet. Now you won't mind if I go away slow? It's no more'n fair, seein' I'll be out of sight inside a hundred yards." —Madge agreed, and added, "And I promise you faithfully that we won't do anything to influence him."

"Well, then, I might as well be gettin' along," Skiff Miller said in the ordinary tones of one departing.

At this change in his voice, Wolf lifted his head quickly, and still more quickly got to his feet when the man and woman shook hands. He sprang up on his hind legs, resting his fore paws on her hip and at the same time licking Skiff Miller's hand. When the latter shook hands with Walt, Wolf repeated his act, resting his weight on Walt and licking both men's hands.

"It ain't no picnic, I can tell you that," were the Klondiker's last words, as he turned and went slowly up the trail.

For the distance of twenty feet Wolf watched him go, himself all eagerness and expectancy, as though waiting for the man to turn and retrace his steps. Then, with a quick low whine, Wolf sprang after him, overtook him, caught his hand between his teeth with reluctant tenderness, and strove gently to make him pause.

Failing in this, Wolf raced back to where Walt Irvine sat, catching his coat-sleeve in his teeth and trying vainly to drag him after the retreating man.

Wolf's perturbation began to wax. He desired ubiquity. He wanted to be in two places at the same time, with the old master and the new, and steadily the distance between them was increasing. He sprang about excitedly, making short nervous leaps and twists, now toward one, now toward the other, in painful indecision, not knowing his own mind, desiring both and unable to choose, uttering quick sharp whines and beginning to pant.

He sat down abruptly on his haunches, thrusting his nose upward, the mouth opening and closing with jerking movements, each time opening wider. These jerking movements were in unison with the recurrent spasms that attacked the throat, each spasm severer and more intense than the preceding one. And in accord with jerks and spasms the larynx began to vibrate, at first silently, accompanied by the rush of air expelled from the lungs, then sounding a low, deep note, the lowest in the register of the human ear. All this was the nervous and muscular preliminary to howling.

But just as the howl was on the verge of bursting from the full throat, the wide-opened mouth was closed, the paroxysms ceased, and he looked long and steadily at the retreating man. Suddenly Wolf turned his head, and over his shoulder just as steadily regarded Walt. The appeal was unanswered. Not a word nor a sign did the dog receive, no suggestion and no clue as to what his conduct should be.

A glance ahead to where the old master was nearing the curve of the trail excited him again. He sprang to his feet with a whine, and then, struck by a new idea, turned his attention to Madge. Hitherto he had ignored her, but now, both masters failing him, she alone was left. He went over to her and snuggled his head in her lap, nudging her arm with his nose—an old trick of his when begging for favors. He backed away from her and began writhing and twisting playfully, curveting and prancing, half rearing and striking his fore paws to the earth, struggling with all his body, from the wheedling eyes and flattening ears to the wagging tail, to express the thought that was in him and that was denied him utterance.

This, too, he soon abandoned. He was depressed by the coldness of these humans who had never been cold before. No response could he draw from them, no help could he get. They did not consider him. They were as dead.

He turned and silently gazed after the old master. Skiff Miller was rounding the curve. In a moment he would be gone from view. Yet he never turned his head, plodding straight onward, slowly and methodically, as though possessed of no interest in what was occurring behind his back.

And in this fashion he went out of view. Wolf waited for him to reappear. He waited a long minute, silently, quietly, without movement, as though turned to stone—withal stone quick with eagerness and desire. He barked once, and waited. Then he turned and trotted back to Walt Irvine. He sniffed his hand and dropped down heavily at his feet, watching the trail where it curved emptily from view.

The tiny stream slipping down the mossy-lipped stone seemed suddenly to increase the volume of its gurgling noise. Save for the meadow-larks, there was no other sound. The great yellow butterflies drifted silently through the sunshine and lost themselves in the drowsy shadows. Madge gazed triumphantly at her husband.

A few minutes later Wolf got upon his feet. Decision and deliberation marked his movements. He did not glance at the man and woman. His eyes were fixed up the trail. He had made up his mind. They knew it. And they knew, so far as they were concerned, that the ordeal had just begun.

He broke into a trot, and Madge's lips pursed, forming an avenue for the caressing sound that it was the will of her to send forth. But the caressing sound was not made. She was impelled to look at her husband, and she saw the sternness with which he watched her. The pursed lips relaxed, and she sighed inaudibly.

Wolf's trot broke into a run. Wider and wider were the leaps he made. Not once did he turn his head, his wolf's brush standing out straight behind him. He cut sharply across the curve of the trail and was gone.

A Yellow Dog

[BRET HARTE]

I never knew why in the Western States of America a yellow dog should be proverbially considered the acme of canine degradation and incompetency, nor why the possession of one should seriously affect the social standing of its possessor. But the fact being established, I think we accepted it at Rattlers Ridge without question. The matter of ownership was more difficult to settle; and although the dog I have in my mind at the present writing attached himself impartially and equally to everyone in camp, no one ventured to exclusively claim him; while, after the perpetration of any canine atrocity, everybody repudiated him with indecent haste.

"Well, I can swear he hasn't been near our shanty for weeks," or the retort, "He was last seen comin' out of *your* cabin," expressed the eagerness with which Rattlers Ridge washed its hands of any responsibility. Yet he was by no means a common dog, nor even an unhandsome dog; and it was a singular fact that his severest critics vied with each other in narrating instances of his sagacity, insight, and agility which they themselves had witnessed.

He had been seen crossing the "flume" that spanned Grizzly Canyon at a height of nine hundred feet, on a plank six inches wide. He had tumbled down the "shoot" to the South Fork, a thousand feet below, and was found sitting on the riverbank "without a scratch, 'cept that he was lazily givin' himself with his off hind paw." He had been forgotten in a snowdrift on a Sierran shelf, and had come home in the early spring with the conceited complacency of an Alpine traveler and a plumpness alleged to have been the result of an exclusive diet of buried mail bags and their contents. He was generally believed to read the advance election posters, and disappear a day or two before the candidates and the brass band—which he hated—came to the Ridge. He was suspected of having overlooked Colonel Johnson's hand at poker, and of having conveyed to the Colonel's adversary, by a succession of barks, the danger of betting against four kings.

While these statements were supplied by wholly unsupported witnesses, it was a very human weakness of Rattlers Ridge that the responsibility of corroboration was passed to the dog himself, and HE was looked upon as a consummate liar.

"Snoopin' round yere, and *callin'* yourself a poker sharp, are ye! Scoot, you yaller pizin!" was a common adjuration whenever the unfortunate animal intruded upon a card party. "Ef thar was a spark, an *atom* of truth in *that dog,* I'd believe my own eyes that I saw him sittin' up and trying to magnetize a jay bird off a tree. But wot are ye goin' to do with a yaller equivocator like that?"

I have said that he was yellow—or, to use the ordinary expression, "yaller." Indeed, I am inclined to believe that much of the ignominy attached to the epithet lay in this favorite pronunciation. Men who habitually spoke of a "*yellow* bird," a "*yellow*-hammer," a "*yellow* leaf," always alluded to him as a "*yaller* dog."

He certainly *was* yellow. After a bath—usually compulsory—he presented a decided gamboge streak down his back, from the top of his forehead to the stump of his tail, fading in his sides and flank to a delicate straw color. His breast, legs, and feet—when not reddened by "slumgullion," in which he was fond of wading—were white. A few attempts at ornamental decoration from the India-ink pot of the storekeeper failed, partly through the yellow dog's excessive agility, which would never give the paint time to dry on him, and partly through his success in transferring his markings to the trousers and blankets of the camp.

The size and shape of his tail—which had been cut off before his introduction to Rattlers Ridge—were favorite sources of speculation to the miners, as determining both his breed and his moral responsibility in coming into camp in that defective condition. There was a general opinion that he couldn't have looked worse with a tail, and its removal was therefore a gratuitous effrontery.

His best feature was his eyes, which were a lustrous Vandyke brown, and sparkling with intelligence; but here again he suffered from evolution through environment, and their original trustful openness was marred by the experience of watching for flying stones, sods, and passing kicks from the rear, so that the pupils were continually reverting to the outer angle of the eyelid.

Nevertheless, none of these characteristics decided the vexed question of his *breed*. His speed and scent pointed to a "hound," and it is related that on one occasion he was laid on the trail of a wildcat with such success that he followed it apparently out of the State, returning at the end of two weeks footsore, but blandly contented.

Attaching himself to a prospecting party, he was sent under the same belief, "into the brush" to drive

off a bear, who was supposed to be haunting the
campfire. He returned in a few minutes *with* the
bear, *driving it into* the unarmed circle and scattering
the whole party. After this the theory of his being a
hunting dog was abandoned. Yet it was said—on
the usual uncorroborated evidence—that he had
"put up" a quail; and his qualities as a retriever were
for a long time accepted, until, during a shooting
expedition for wild ducks, it was discovered that the
one he had brought back had never been shot, and
the party were obliged to compound damages with
an adjacent settler.

His fondness for paddling in the ditches and
"slumgullion" at one time suggested a water spaniel.
He could swim, and would occasionally bring out of
the river sticks and pieces of bark that had been
thrown in; but as *he* always had to be thrown in with
them, and was a good-sized dog, his aquatic reputation faded also. He remained simply "a yaller dog."
What more could be said? His actual name was
"Bones"—given to him, no doubt, through the
provincial custom of confounding the occupation of
the individual with his quality, for which it was
pointed out precedent could be found in some old
English family names.

But if Bones generally exhibited no preference
for any particular individual in camp, he always
made an exception in favor of drunkards. Even an

ordinary roistering bacchanalian party brought him out from under a tree or a shed in the keenest satisfaction. He would accompany them through the long straggling street of the settlement, barking his delight at every step or misstep of the revelers, and exhibiting none of that mistrust of eye which marked his attendance upon the sane and the respectable. He accepted even their uncouth play without a snarl or a yelp, hypocritically pretending even to like it; and I conscientiously believe would have allowed a tin can to be attached to his tail if the hand that tied it on were only unsteady, and the voice that bade him "lie still" were husky with liquor. He would "see" the party cheerfully into a saloon, wait outside the door—his tongue fairly lolling from his mouth in enjoyment—until they reappeared, permit them even to tumble over him with pleasure, and then gambol away before them, heedless of awkwardly projected stones and epithets. He would afterward accompany them separately home, or lie with them at crossroads until they were assisted to their cabins. Then he would trot rakishly to his own haunt by the saloon stove, with the slightly conscious air of having been a bad dog, yet of having had a good time.

We never could satisfy ourselves whether his enjoyment arose from some merely selfish conviction that he was more *secure* with the physically and mentally incompetent, from some active sympathy with active wickedness, or from a grim sense of his own mental superiority at such moments. But the general belief leant toward his kindred sympathy as a "yaller dog" with all that was disreputable. And this was supported by another very singular canine manifestation—the "sincere flattery" of simulation or imitation.

"Uncle Billy" Riley for a short time enjoyed the position of being the camp drunkard, and at once became an object of Bones' greatest solicitude. He not only accompanied him everywhere, curled at his feet or head according to Uncle Billy's attitude at the moment, but, it was noticed, began presently to undergo a singular alteration in his own habits and appearance. From being an active, tireless scout and forager, a bold and unovertakable marauder, he became lazy and apathetic; allowed gophers to burrow under him without endeavoring to undermine the settlement in his frantic endeavors to dig them out, permitted squirrels to flash their tails at him a hundred yards away, forgot his usual caches, and left his favorite bones unburied and bleaching in the sun. His eyes grew dull, his coat lusterless, in proportion as his companion became blear-eyed and ragged; in running, his usual arrowlike directness began to deviate, and it was not unusual to meet the pair together, zigzagging up the hill. Indeed, Uncle

Billy's condition could be predetermined by Bones' appearance at times when his temporary master was invisible. "The old man must have an awful jag on today," was casually remarked when an extra fluffiness and imbecility was noticeable in the passing Bones. At first it was believed that he drank also, but when careful investigation proved this hypothesis untenable, he was freely called a "derned time—servin', yaller hypocrite." Not a few advanced the opinion that if Bones did not actually lead Uncle Billy astray, he at least "slavered him over and coddled him until the old man got conceited in his wickedness." This undoubtedly led to a compulsory divorce between them, and Uncle Billy was happily dispatched to a neighboring town and a doctor.

Bones seemed to miss him greatly, ran away for two days, and was supposed to have visited him, to have been shocked at his convalescence, and to have been "cut" by Uncle Billy in his reformed character; and he returned to his old active life again, and buried his past with his forgotten bones. It was said that he was afterward detected in trying to lead an intoxicated tramp into camp after the methods employed by a blind man's dog, but was discovered in time by the— of course—uncorroborated narrator.

I should be tempted to leave him thus in his original and picturesque sin, but the same veracity which compelled me to transcribe his faults and iniquities obliges me to describe his ultimate and somewhat monotonous reformation, which came from no fault of his own.

It was a joyous day at Rattlers Ridge that was equally the advent of his change of heart and the first stagecoach that had been induced to diverge from the highroad and stop regularly at our settlement. Flags were flying from the post office and Polka saloon, and Bones was flying before the brass band that he detested, when the sweetest girl in the county—Pinkey Preston—daughter of the county judge and hopelessly beloved by all Rattlers Ridge, stepped from the coach which she had glorified by occupying as an invited guest.

"What makes him run away?" she asked quickly, opening her lovely eyes in a possibly innocent wonder that anything could be found to run away from her.

"He don't like the brass band," we explained eagerly.

"How funny," murmured the girl; "is it as out of tune as all that?"

This irresistible witticism alone would have been enough to satisfy us—we did nothing but repeat it to each other all the next day—but we were positively transported when we saw her suddenly gather her dainty skirts in one hand and trip off through the red dust toward Bones, who, with his eyes over his yellow shoulder, had halted in the road, and half-turned in mingled disgust and rage at the spectacle of the descending trombone. We held our breath as she approached him. Would Bones evade her as he did us at such moments, or would he save our reputation, and consent, for the moment, to accept her as a new kind of inebriate? She came nearer; he saw her; he began to slowly quiver with excitement—his stump of a tail vibrating with such rapidity that the loss of the missing portion was scarcely noticeable. Suddenly she stopped before him, took his yellow head between her little hands, lifted it, and looked down in his handsome brown eyes with her two lovely blue ones. What passed between them in that magnetic glance no one ever knew. She returned with him; said to him casually: "We're not afraid of brass bands, are we?" to which he apparently acquiesced, at least stifling his disgust of them while he was near her—which was nearly all the time.

During the speechmaking her gloved hand and his yellow head were always near together, and at the crowning ceremony—her public checking of Yuba Bill's "waybill" on behalf of the township, with a gold pencil presented to her by the Stage Company—Bones' joy, far from knowing no bounds, seemed to know nothing but them, and he witnessed it apparently in the air. No one dared to interfere.

For the first time a local pride in Bones sprang up in our hearts—and we lied to each other in his praises openly and shamelessly.

Then the time came for parting. We were standing by the door of the coach, hats in hand, as Miss Pinkey was about to step into it; Bones was waiting by her side, confidently looking into the interior, and apparently selecting his own seat on the lap of Judge Preston in the corner, when Miss Pinkey held up the sweetest of admonitory fingers. Then, taking his head between her two hands, she again looked into his brimming eyes, and said, simply, "*good* dog," with the gentlest of emphasis on the adjective, and popped into the coach.

The six bay horses started as one, the gorgeous green and gold vehicle bounded forward, the red dust rose behind, and the yellow dog danced in and out of it to the very outskirts of the settlement. And then he soberly returned.

A day or two later he was missed—but the fact was afterward known that he was at Spring Valley, the county town where Miss Preston lived, and he was forgiven. A week afterward he was missed again, but this time for a longer period, and then a pathetic letter arrived from Sacramento for the storekeeper's wife.

"Would you mind," wrote Miss Pinkey Preston, "asking some of your boys to come over here to

Sacramento and bring back Bones? I don't mind having the dear dog walk out with me at Spring Valley, where everyone knows me; but here he *does* make one so noticeable, on account of *his color.* I've got scarcely a frock that he agrees with. He don't go with my pink muslin, and that lovely buff tint he makes three shades lighter. You know yellow is *so* trying."

A consultation was quickly held by the whole settlement, and a deputation sent to Sacramento to relieve the unfortunate girl. We were all quite indignant with Bones—but, oddly enough, I think it was greatly tempered with our new pride in him. While he was with us alone, his peculiarities had been scarcely appreciated, but the recurrent phrase "that yellow dog that they keep at the Rattlers" gave us a mysterious importance along the countryside, as if we had secured a "mascot" in some zoological curiosity.

This was further indicated by a singular occurrence. A new church had been built at the crossroads, and an eminent divine had come from San Francisco to preach the opening sermon. After a careful examination of the camp's wardrobe, and some felicitous exchange of apparel, a few of us were deputed to represent "Rattlers" at the Sunday service. In our white ducks, straw hats, and flannel blouses, we were sufficiently picturesque

and distinctive as "honest miners" to be shown off
in one of the front pews.

Seated near the prettiest girls, who offered us
their hymn books—in the cleanly odor of fresh
pine shavings, and ironed muslin, and blown over
by the spices of our own woods through the open
windows, a deep sense of the abiding peace of
Christian communion settled upon us. At this
supreme moment someone murmured in an awe-
stricken whisper:

"*Will* you look at Bones?"

We looked. Bones had entered the church and
gone up in the gallery through a pardonable ignorance and modesty; but, perceiving his mistake, was
now calmly walking along the gallery rail before
the astounded worshipers. Reaching the end, he
paused for a moment, and carelessly looked down.
It was about fifteen feet to the floor below—the
simplest jump in the world for the mountain-bred
Bones. Daintily, gingerly, lazily, and yet with a conceited airiness of manner, as if, humanly speaking,
he had one leg in his pocket and were doing it on
three, he cleared the distance, dropping just in
front of the chancel, without a sound, turned himself around three times, and then lay comfortably
down.

Three deacons were instantly in the aisle, coming
up before the eminent divine, who, we fancied, wore

a restrained smile. We heard the hurried whispers: "Belongs to them." "Quite a local institution here, you know." "Don't like to offend sensibilities"; and the minister's prompt "By no means," as he went on with his service.

A short month ago we would have repudiated Bones; today we sat there in slightly supercilious attitudes, as if to indicate that any affront offered to Bones would be an insult to ourselves, and followed by our instantaneous withdrawal in a body.

All went well, however, until the minister, lifting the large Bible from the communion table and holding it in both hands before him, walked toward a reading stand by the altar rails. Bones uttered a distinct growl. The minister stopped.

We, and we alone, comprehended in a flash the whole situation. The Bible was nearly the size and shape of one of those soft clods of sod which we were in the playful habit of launching at Bones when he lay half-asleep in the sun, in order to see him cleverly evade it.

We held our breath. What was to be done? But the opportunity belonged to our leader, Jeff Briggs—a confoundedly good-looking fellow, with the golden mustache of a northern Viking and the curls of an Apollo. Secure in his beauty and bland in his self-conceit, he rose from the pew, and stepped before the chancel rails.

"I would wait a moment, if I were you, sir," he said, respectfully, "and you will see that he will go out quietly."

"What is wrong?" whispered the minister in some concern.

"He thinks you are going to heave that book at him, sir, without giving him a fair show, as we do."

The minister looked perplexed, but remained motionless, with the book in his hands. Bones arose, walked halfway down the aisle, and vanished like a yellow flash!

With this justification of his reputation, Bones disappeared for a week. At the end of that time we received a polite note from Judge Preston, saying that the dog had become quite domiciled in their house, and begged that the camp, without yielding up their valuable *property* in him, would allow him to remain at Spring Valley for an indefinite time; that both the judge and his daughter—with whom Bones was already an old friend—would be glad if the members of the camp would visit their old favorite whenever they desired, to assure themselves that he was well cared for.

I am afraid that the bait thus ingenuously thrown out had a good deal to do with our ultimate yielding. However, the reports of those who visited Bones were wonderful and marvelous. He was residing there in state, lying on rugs in the drawing-room, coiled up under the judicial desk in the judge's study, sleeping regularly on the mat outside Miss Pinkey's bedroom door, or lazily snapping at flies on the judge's lawn.

"He's as yaller as ever," said one of our informants, "but it don't somehow seem to be the same back that we used to break clods over in the old time, just to see him scoot out of the dust."

And now I must record a fact which I am aware all lovers of dogs will indignantly deny, and which will be furiously bayed at by every faithful hound since the days of Ulysses. Bones not only *forgot,* but absolutely *cut us*! Those who called upon the judge in "store clothes" he would perhaps casually notice, but he would sniff at them as if detecting and resenting them under their superficial exterior. The rest he simply paid no attention to. The more familiar term of "Bonesy"—formerly applied to him, as in our rare moments of endearment—produced no response. This pained, I think, some of the more youthful of us; but, through some strange human weakness, it also increased the camp's respect for him. Nevertheless, we spoke of him familiarly to strangers at the very moment he ignored us. I am afraid that we also took some pains to point out that he was getting fat and unwieldy, and losing his elasticity, implying covertly that his choice was a mistake and his life a failure.

A year after, he died, in the odor of sanctity and respectability, being found one morning coiled up and stiff on the mat outside Miss Pinkey's door. When the news was conveyed to us, we asked permission, the camp being in a prosperous condition, to erect a stone over his grave. But when it came to the inscription we could only think of the two words murmured to him by Miss Pinkey, which we always believe effected his conversion:

"*Good* Dog!"

Bingo

[ERNEST THOMPSON SETON]

"Ye Franckelyn's dogge leaped over a style,
And yey yclept him lyttel Bingo,
   B-I-N-G-O,

And yey yclept him lyttel Bingo.
Ye Franckelyn's wyfe brewed nutte-brown ayle,
And he yclept ytte rare-goode Stingo,
   S-T-I-N-G-O,

And he yclept ytte rare goode Stingo.
Now ys not this a prettye rhyme,
I thynke ytte ys bye Jingo,
   J-I-N-G-O,
I thynke ytte ys bye Jingo."

I

It was early in November 1882, and the Manitoba winter had just set in. I was tilting back in my chair for a few lazy moments after breakfast, idly alternating my gaze from the one window-pane of our shanty, through which was framed a bit of the prairie and the end of our cowshed, to the old rhyme of the "Franckelyn's dogge" pinned on the logs near by. But the dreamy mixture of rhyme and view was quickly dispelled by the sight of a large gray animal dashing across the prairie into the cowshed, with a smaller black and white animal in hot pursuit.

"A wolf," I exclaimed, and seizing a rifle dashed out to help the dog. But before I could get there they had left the stable, and after a short run over the snow the wolf again turned at bay, and the dog, our neighbor's collie, circled about watching his chance to snap.

I fired a couple of long shots, which had the effect only of setting them off again over the prairie. After another run this matchless dog closed and seized the wolf by the haunch, but again retreated to avoid the fierce return chop. Then there was another stand at bay, and again a race over the snow. Every few hundred yards this scene was repeated, the dog managing so that each fresh rush should be toward the settlement, while the wolf vainly tried to break back toward the dark belt of trees in the east. At last after a mile of this fighting and running I overtook them, and the dog, seeing that he now had good backing, closed in for the finish.

After a few seconds the whirl of struggling animals resolved itself into a wolf, on his back, with a bleeding collie gripping his throat, and it was now easy for me to step up and end the fight by putting a ball through the wolf's head.

Then, when this dog of marvelous wind saw that his foe was dead, he gave him no second glance, but set out at a lope for a farm four miles across the snow where he had left his master when first the wolf was started. He was a wonderful dog, and even if I had not come he undoubtedly would have killed the wolf alone, as I learned he had already done with others of the kind, in spite of the fact that the wolf, though of the smaller or prairie race, was much larger than himself. I was filled with admiration for the dog's prowess and at once sought to buy him at any price. The scornful reply of his owner was, "Why don't you try to buy one of the children?"

Since Frank was not in the market I was obliged to content myself with the next best thing, one of his alleged progeny. That is, a son of his wife. This probable offspring of an illustrious sire was a roly-poly ball of black fur that looked more like a long-tailed bear cub than a puppy. But he had some tan markings like those on Frank's coat, that were, I hoped, guarantees of future greatness, and also a very characteristic ring of white that he always wore on his muzzle.

Having got possession of his person, the next thing was to find him a name. Surely this puzzle was already solved. The rhyme of the "Franckelyn's dogge" was in-built with the foundation of our acquaintance, so with adequate pomp we "yclept him little Bingo."

II

The rest of that winter Bingo spent in our shanty, living the life of a blubbery, fat, well-meaning, ill-doing puppy; gorging himself with food and growing bigger and clumsier each day. Even sad experience failed to teach him that he must keep his nose out of the rattrap. His most friendly overtures to the cat were wholly misunderstood and resulted only in an armed neutrality that varied by occasional reigns of terror, continued to the end; which came when Bingo, who early showed a mind of his own, got a notion for sleeping at the barn and avoiding the shanty altogether.

When the spring came I set about his serious education. After much pains on my behalf and many pains on his, he learned to go at the word in quest of our old yellow cow, that pastured at will on the unfenced prairie.

Once he had learned his business, he became very fond of it and nothing pleased him more than an order to go and fetch the cow. Away he would dash, barking with pleasure and leaping high in the air that he might better scan the plain for his victim. In a short time he would return driving her at full gallop before him, and gave her no peace until, puffing and blowing, she was safely driven into the farthest corner of her stable.

Less energy on his part would have been more satisfactory, but we bore with him until he grew so fond of this semi-daily hunt that he began to bring "old Dunne" without being told. And at length not once or twice but a dozen times a day this energetic cowherd would sally forth on his own responsibility and drive the cow home to the stable.

At last things came to such a pass that whenever he felt like taking a little exercise, or had a few minutes of spare time, or even happened to think of it, Bingo would sally forth at racing speed over the plain and a few minutes later return, driving the unhappy yellow cow at full gallop before him.

At first this did not seem very bad, as it kept the cow from straying too far; but soon it was seen that it hindered her feeding. She became thin and gave less milk; it seemed to weigh on her mind too, as she was always watching nervously for that hateful dog, and in the mornings would hang around the stable as though afraid to venture off and subject herself at once to an onset.

This was going too far. All attempts to make Bingo more moderate in his pleasure were failures, so he was compelled to give it up altogether. After this, though he dared not bring her home, he continued to show his interest by lying at her stable door while she was being milked.

As the summer came on the mosquitoes became a dreadful plague, and the consequent vicious switching of Dunne's tail at milking-time was even more annoying than the mosquitoes.

Fred, the brother who did the milking, was of an inventive as well as an impatient turn of mind, and he devised a simple plan to stop the switching. He fastened a brick to the cow's tail, then set blithely about his work assured of unusual comfort while the rest of us looked on in doubt.

Suddenly through the mist of mosquitoes came a dull whack and an outburst of "language." The cow went on placidly chewing till Fred got on his feet and furiously attacked her with the milking-stool. It was bad enough to be whacked on the ear with a brick by a stupid old cow, but the uproarious enjoyment and ridicule of the bystanders made it unendurable. Bingo, hearing the uproar, and divining that he was needed, rushed in and attacked Dunne on the other side. Before the affair quieted down the milk was spilt, the pail and stool were broken, and the cow and the dog severely beaten.

Poor Bingo could not understand it at all. He had long ago learned to despise that cow, and now in utter disgust he decided to forsake even her stable door, and from that time be attached himself exclusively to the horses and their stable.

The cattle were mine, the horses were my brother's, and in transferring his allegiance from the cow-stable to the horse-stable Bingo seemed to give me up too, and anything like daily companionship ceased, and yet, whenever any emergency arose Bingo turned to me and I to him, and both seemed to feel that the bond between man and dog is one that lasts as long as life.

The only other occasion on which Bingo acted as cowherd was in the autumn of the same year at the annual Carberry Fair. Among the dazzling inducements to enter one's stock there was, in addition to a prospect of glory, a cash prize of "two dollars" for the "best collie in training."

Misled by a false friend, I entered Bingo, and early on the day fixed, the cow was driven to the prairie just outside of the village. When the time came she was pointed out to Bingo and the word given—"Go fetch the cow." It was the intention, of course, that he should bring her to me at the judge's stand.

But the animals knew better. They hadn't rehearsed all summer for nothing. When Dunne saw Bingo's careering form she knew that her only hope for safety was to get into her stable, and Bingo was equally sure that his sole mission in life was to quicken her pace in that direction. So off they raced over the prairie, like a wolf after a deer, and heading straight toward their home two miles away, they disappeared from view.

That was the last that judge or jury ever saw of dog or cow. The prize was awarded to the only other entry.

III

Bingo's loyalty to the horses was quite remarkable; by day he trotted beside them, and by night he slept at the stable door. Where the team went Bingo went, and nothing kept him away from them. This interesting assumption of ownership lent the greater significance to the following circumstance.

I was not superstitious, and up to this time had had no faith in omens, but was now deeply impressed by a strange occurrence in which Bingo took a leading part. There were but two of us now living on the De Winton Farm. One morning my brother set out for Boggy Creek for a load of hay. It was a long day's journey there and back, and he made an early start.

Strange to tell, Bingo for once in his life did not follow the team. My brother called to him, but still he
stood at a safe distance, and eyeing the team askance,
refused to stir. Suddenly he raised his nose in the air
and gave vent to a long, melancholy howl. He
watched the wagon out of sight, and even followed
for a hundred yards or so, raising his voice from time
to time in the most doleful howlings.

All that day he stayed about the barn, the only
time that he was willingly separated from the horses,
and at intervals howled a very death dirge. I was
alone, and the dog's behavior inspired me with an
awful foreboding of calamity, that weighed upon use
more and more as the hours passed away.

About six o'clock Bingo's howlings became
unbearable, so that for lack of a better thought I
threw something at him, and ordered him away.
But oh, the feeling of horror that filled me. Why
did I let my brother go away alone? Should I ever
again see him alive? I might have known from the
dog's actions that something dreadful was about to
happen.

At length the hour for his return arrived, and there
was John on his load. I took charge of the horses,
vastly relieved, and with an air of assumed uncon-
cern, asked, "All right?"

"Right," was the laconic answer.

Who now can say that there is nothing in omens.

And yet when, long afterward, I told this to one skilled in the occult, he looked grave, and said, "Bingo always turned to you in a crisis?"

"Yes."

"Then do not smile. It was you that were in danger that day; he stayed and saved your life, though you never knew from what."

IV

Early in the spring I had begun Bingo's education. Very shortly afterward he began mine.

Midway on the two-mile stretch of prairie that lay between our shanty and the village of Carberry, was the corner-stake of the farm; it was a stout post in a low mound of earth, and was visible from afar.

I soon noticed that Bingo never passed without minutely examining this mysterious post. Next I learned that it was also visited by the prairie wolves as well as by all the dogs in the neighborhood, and at length, with the aid of a telescope, I made a number of observations that helped me to an understanding of the matter and enabled me to enter more fully into Bingo's private life.

The post was by common agreement a registry of the canine tribes. Their exquisite sense of smell enabled each individual to tell at once by the track and trace what other had recently been at the post.

When the snow came much more was revealed. I then discovered that this post was but one of a system that covered the country; that, in short, the entire region was laid out in signal stations at convenient intervals. These were marked by any conspicuous post, stone, buffalo skull, or other object that chanced to be in the desired locality, and extensive observation showed that it was a very complete system for getting and giving the news.

Each dog or wolf makes a point of calling at those stations that are near his line of travel to learn who has recently been there, just as a man calls at his club on returning to town and looks up the register.

I have seen Bingo approach the post, sniff, examine the ground about, then growl, and with bristling mane and glowing eyes, scratch fiercely and contemptuously with his hind feet, finally walking off very stiffly, glancing back from time to time. All of which, being interpreted, said:

"*Grrrh! woof!* there's that dirty cur of McCarthy's. *Woof!* I'll 'tend to him tonight. *Woof! woof!*"

On another occasion, after the preliminaries, he became keenly interested and studied a coyote's track that came and went, saying to himself, as I afterward learned:

"A coyote track coming from the north, smelling of dead cow. Indeed? Pollworth's old Brindle must be dead at last. This is worth looking into."

At other times he would wag his tail, trot about the vicinity and come again and again to make his own visit more evident, perhaps for the benefit of his brother Bill just back from Brandon! So that it was not by chance that one night Bill turned up at Bingo's home and was taken to the hills, where a delicious dead horse afforded a chance to suitably celebrate the reunion.

At other times he would be suddenly aroused by the news, take up the trail, and race to the next station for later information.

Sometimes his inspection produced only an air of grave attention, as though he said to himself, "Dear me, who the deuce is this?" or "It seems to me I met that fellow at the Portage last summer."

One morning on approaching the post Bingo's every hair stood on end, his tail dropped and quivered, and he gave proof that he was suddenly sick at the stomach, sure signs of terror. He showed no desire to follow up or know more of the matter, but returned to the house, and half an hour afterward his mane was still bristling and his expression one of hate or fear.

I studied the dreaded track and learned that in Bingo's language the half-terrified, deep-gurgled *grr-wff* means "timber wolf."

These were among the things that Bingo taught me. And in the after time when I might chance to see him arouse from his frosty nest by the stable door, and after stretching himself and shaking the snow from his shaggy coat, disappear into the gloom at a steady trot, trot, trot, I used to think:

"Ahh! old dog, I know where you are off to, and why you eschew the shelter of the shanty. Now I know why your nightly trips over the country are so well timed, and how you know just where to go for what you want, and when and how to seek it."

V

In the autumn of 1884, the shanty at De Winton farm was closed and Bingo changed his home to the establishment—that is, to the stable, not the house—of Gordon Wright, our most intimate neighbor.

Since the winter of his puppyhood he had declined to enter a house at any time excepting during a thunderstorm. Of thunder and guns he had a deep dread—no doubt the fear of the first originated in the second, and that arose from some unpleasant shotgun experiences, the cause of which will be seen. His nightly couch was outside the stable, even during the coldest weather, and it was easy to see he enjoyed to the full the complete nocturnal liberty entailed. Bingo's midnight wanderings extended across the plains for miles. There was plenty of proof of this. Some farmers at very remote points sent word to old Gordon that if he did not keep his dog home nights, they would use the shotgun, and Bingo's terror of firearms would indicate that the threats were not idle. A man living as far away as Petrel said he saw a large black wolf kill a coyote on the snow one winter evening, but afterward he changed his opinion and "reckoned it must 'a' been Wright's dog." Whenever the body of a winterkilled ox or horse was exposed, Bingo was sure to repair to it nightly, and driving away the prairie wolves, feast to repletion.

Sometimes the object of a night foray was merely to maul some distant neighbor's dog, and notwithstanding vengeful threats, there seemed no reason to fear that the Bingo breed would die out. One man even avowed that he had seen a prairie wolf accompanied by three young ones which resembled the mother, excepting that they were very large and black and had a ring of white around the muzzle.

True or not as that may be, I know that late in March, while we were out in the sleigh with Bingo trotting behind, a prairie wolf was started from a hollow. Away it went with Bingo in full chase, but the wolf did not greatly exert itself to escape, and within a short distance Bingo was close up, yet strange to tell, there was no grappling, no fight!

Bingo trotted amiably alongside and licked the wolf's nose.

We were astounded, and shouted to urge Bingo on. Our shouting and approach several times started the wolf off at speed and Bingo again pursued until he had overtaken it, but his gentleness was too obvious.

"It is a she-wolf, he won't harm her," I exclaimed as the truth dawned on me. And Gordon said: "Well, I be darned."

So we called our unwilling dog and drove on.

For weeks after this we were annoyed by the depredations of a prairie wolf who killed our chickens, stole pieces of pork from the end of the house, and several times terrified the children by looking into the window of the shanty while the men were away.

Against this animal Bingo seemed to be no safeguard. At length the wolf, a female, was killed, and then Bingo plainly showed his hand by his lasting enmity toward Oliver, the man who did the deed.

VI

It is wonderful and beautiful how a man and his dog will stick to one another, through thick and thin. Butler tells of an undivided Indian tribe, in the Far North which was all but exterminated by an internecine feud over a dog that belonged to one man and was killed by his neighbor; and among ourselves we have lawsuits, fights, and deadly feuds, all pointing the same old moral, "Love me, love my dog."

One of our neighbors had a very fine hound that he thought the best and dearest dog in the world. I loved him, so I loved his dog, and when one day poor Tan crawled home terribly mangled and died by the door, I joined my threats of vengeance with those of his master and thenceforth lost no opportunity of tracing the miscreant, both by offering rewards and by collecting scraps of evidence. At length it was clear that one of three men to the southward had had a hand in the cruel affair. The scent was warming up, and soon we should have been in a position to exact rigorous justice, at least, from the wretch who had murdered poor old Tan.

Then something took place which at once changed my mind and led me to believe that the mangling of the old hound was not by any means an unpardonable crime, but indeed on second thoughts was rather commendable than otherwise.

Gordon Wright's farm lay to the south of us, and while there one day, Gordon Jr., knowing that I was tracking the murderer, took me aside and looking about furtively, he whispered, in tragic tones:

"It was Bing done it."

And the matter dropped right there. For I confess that from that moment I did all in my power to baffle the justice I had previously striven so hard to further.

I had given Bingo away long before, but the feeling of ownership did not die; and of this indissoluble fellowship of dog and man he was soon to take part in another important illustration.

Old Gordon and Oliver were close neighbors and friends; they joined in a contract to cut wood, and worked together harmoniously till late on in winter. Then Oliver's old horse died, and he, determining to profit as far as possible, dragged it out on the plain and laid poison baits for wolves around it. Alas for poor Bingo! He would lead a wolfish life, though again and again it brought him into wolfish misfortunes.

He was as fond of dead horse as any of his wild kindred. That very night, with Wright's own dog Curley, he visited the carcass. It seemed as though Bing had busied himself chiefly keeping off the wolves, but Curley feasted immoderately. The tracks in the snow told the story of the banquet; the interruption as the poison began to work, and of the dreadful spasms of pain during the erratic course back home where Curley, falling in convulsions at Gordon's feet, died in the greatest agony.

"Love me, love my dog." No explanations or apology were acceptable; it was useless to urge that it was accidental; the long-standing feud between Bingo and Oliver was now remembered as an important sidelight. The wood-contract was thrown up, all friendly relations ceased, and to this day there is no county big enough to hold the rival factions which were called at once into existence and to arms by Curley's dying yell.

It was months before Bingo really recovered from the poison. We believed indeed that he never again would be the sturdy old-time Bingo. But when the spring came he began to gain strength, and bettering as the grass grew, he was within a few weeks once more in full health and vigor to be a pride to his friends and a nuisance to his neighbors.

VII

Changes took me far away from Manitoba, and on my return in 1886 Bingo was still a member of Wright's household. I thought he would have forgotten me after two years' absence, but not so. One day early in the winter, after having been lost for forty-eight hours, he crawled home to Wright's with a wolf-trap and a heavy log fast to one foot, and the foot frozen to stony hardness. No one had been able to approach to help him, he was so savage, when I, the stranger now, stooped down and laid hold of the trap with one hand and his leg with the other. Instantly he seized my wrist in his teeth.

Without stirring I said, "Bing, don't you know me?"

He had not broken the skin and at once released his hold and offered no further resistance, although he whined a good deal during the removal of the trap. He still acknowledged me his master in spite of his change of residence and my long absence, and notwithstanding my surrender of ownership I still felt that he was my dog.

Bing was carried into the house much against his will and his frozen foot thawed out. During the rest of the winter he went lame and two of his toes eventually dropped off. But before the return of warm weather his health and strength were fully restored, and to a casual glance he bore no mark of his dreadful experience in the steel trap.

VIII

During that same winter I caught many wolves and foxes who did not have Bingo's good luck in escaping the traps, which I kept out right into the spring, for bounties are good even when fur is not.

Kennedy's Plain was always a good trapping ground because it was unfrequented by man and yet lay between the heavy woods and the settlement. I had been fortunate with the fur here, and late in April rode in on one of my regular rounds.

The wolf-traps are made of heavy steel and have two springs, each of one hundred pounds power.

They are set in fours around a buried bait, and after being strongly fastened to concealed logs are carefully covered in cotton and in fine sand so as to be quite invisible. A prairie wolf was caught in one of these. I killed him with a club and throwing him aside proceeded to reset the trap as I had done so many hundred times before. All was quickly done. I threw the trap-wrench over toward the pony, and seeing some fine sand nearby, I reached out for a handful of it to add a good finish to the setting.

Oh, unlucky thought! Oh, mad heedlessness born of long immunity! That fine sand was on the next wolftrap and in an instant I was a prisoner. Although not wounded, for the traps have no teeth, and my thick trapping gloves deadened the snap, I was firmly caught across the hand above the knuckles. Not greatly alarmed at this, I tried to reach the trap-wrench with my right foot. Stretching out at full length, face downward, I worked myself toward it, making my imprisoned arm as long and straight as possible. I could not see and reach at the same time, but counted on my toe telling me when I touched the little iron key to my fetters. My first effort was a failure; strain as I might at the chain my toe struck no metal. I swung slowly around my anchor, but still failed. Then a painfully taken observation showed I was much too far to the west. I set about working around, tapping blindly with my toe to discover the

key. Thus wildly groping with my right foot I forgot about the other till there was a sharp *clank* and the iron jaws of trap No. 5 closed tight on my left foot.

The terrors of the situation did not, at first, impress me, but I soon found that all my struggles were in vain. I could not get free from either trap or move the traps together, and there I lay stretched out and firmly staked to the ground.

What would become of me now? There was not much danger of freezing for the cold weather was over, but Kennedy's Plain was never visited by the winter woodcutters. No one knew where I had gone, and unless I could manage to free myself there was no prospect ahead but to be devoured by wolves, or else die of cold and starvation.

As I lay there the red sun went down over the spruce swamp west of the plain, and a shorelark on a gopher mound a few yards off twittered his evening song, just as one had done the night before at our shanty door, and though the numb pains were creeping up my arm, and a deadly chill possessed me, I noticed how long his little ear-tufts were. Then my thoughts went to the comfortable supper-table at Wright's shanty, and I thought, now they are frying the pork for supper, or just sitting down. My pony still stood as I left him with his bridle on the ground patiently waiting to take me home. He did not understand the long delay, and when I called, he ceased nibbling the grass and looked at me in dumb, helpless inquiry. If he would only go home the empty saddle might tell the tale and bring help. But his very faithfulness kept him waiting hour after hour while I was perishing of cold and hunger.

Then I remembered how old Girou the trapper had been lost, and in the following spring his comrades found his skeleton held by the leg in a beartrap. I wondered which part of my clothing would show my identity. Then a new thought came to me. This is how a wolf feels when he is trapped. Oh! what misery have I been responsible for! Now I'm to pay for it.

Night came slowly on. A prairie wolf howled, the pony pricked up his ears and, walking nearer to me, stood with his head down. Then another prairie wolf howled and another, and I could make out that they were gathering in the neighborhood. There I lay prone and helpless, wondering if it would not be strictly just that they should come and tear me to pieces. I heard them calling for a long time before I realized that dim, shadowy forms were sneaking near. The horse saw them first, and his terrified snort drove them back at first, but they came nearer next time and sat around me on the prairie. Soon one bolder than the others crawled up and tugged at the body of his dead relative. I shouted and he retreated growling. The pony ran to a distance in terror.

Presently the wolf returned, and after two or three of these retreats and returns, the body was dragged off and devoured by the rest in a few minutes.

After this they gathered nearer and sat on their haunches to look at me, and the boldest one smelt the rifle and scratched dirt on it. He retreated when I kicked at him with my free foot and shouted, but growing bolder as I grew weaker he came and snarled right in my face. At this several others snarled and came up closer, and I realized that I was to be devoured by the foe that I most despised; when suddenly out of the gloom with a guttural roar sprang a great black wolf. The prairie wolves scattered like chaff except the bold one, which, seized by the black new-comer, was in a few moments a draggled corpse, and then, oh horrors! this mighty brute bounded at me and—Bingo—noble Bingo, rubbed his shaggy, panting sides against me and licked my cold face.

"Bingo—Bing—old—boy—Fetch me the trap wrench!" Away he went and returned dragging the rifle, for he knew only that I wanted something.

"No—Bing—the trap-wrench." This time it was my sash, but at last he brought the wrench and wagged his tail in joy that it was right. Reaching out with my free hand, after much difficulty I unscrewed the pillar-nut. The trap fell apart and my hand was released, and a minute later I was free. Bing brought the pony up, and after slowly walking to restore the circulation I was able to mount. Then slowly at first but soon at a gallop, with Bingo as herald careering and barking ahead, we set out for home, there to learn that the night before, though never taken on the trapping rounds, the brave dog had acted strangely, whimpering and watching the timber-trail; and at last when night came on, in spite of attempts to detain him he had set out in the gloom and guided by a knowledge that is beyond us had reached the spot in time to avenge me as well as set me free.

Stanch old Bing—he was a strange dog. Though his heart was with me, he passed me next day with scarcely a look, but responded with alacrity when little Gordon called him to a gopher-hunt. And it was so to the end; and to the end also he lived the wolfish life that he loved, and never failed to seek the winter-killed horses and found one again with a poisoned bait, and wolfishly bolted that; then feeling the pang, set out, not for Wright's but to find me, and reached the door of my shanty where I should have been. Next day on returning I found him dead in the snow with his head on the sill of the door—the door of his puppyhood's days; my dog to the last in his heart of hearts—it was my help he sought, and vainly sought, in the hour of his bitter extremity.

A Dark-Brown Dog

[STEPHEN CRANE]

A child was standing on a street-corner. He leaned with one shoulder against a high board fence and swayed the other to and fro, the while kicking carelessly at the gravel.

Sunshine beat upon the cobbles, and a lazy summer wind raised yellow dust which trailed in clouds down the avenue. Clattering trucks moved with indistinctness through it. The child stood dreamily gazing.

After a time, a little dark-brown dog came trotting with an intent air down the sidewalk. A short rope was dragging from his neck. Occasionally he trod upon the end of it and stumbled.

He stopped opposite the child, and the two regarded each other. The dog hesitated for a moment, but presently he made some little advances with his tail.

The child put out his hand and called him. In an apologetic manner the dog came close, and the two had an interchange of friendly pattings and waggles. The dog became more enthusiastic with each moment of the interview, until with his gleeful caperings he threatened to overturn the child. Whereupon the child lifted his hand and struck the dog a blow upon the head.

This thing seemed to overpower and astonish the little dark-brown dog, and wounded him to the heart. He sank down in despair at the child's feet. When the blow was repeated, together with an admonition in childish sentences, he turned over upon his back, and held his paws in a peculiar manner. At the same time with his ears and his eyes he offered a small prayer to the child.

He looked so comical on his back, and holding his paws peculiarly, that the child was greatly amused and gave him little taps repeatedly, to keep him so. But the little dark-brown dog took this chastisement in the most serious way, and no doubt considered that he had committed some grave crime, for he wriggled contritely and showed his repentance in every way that was in his power. He pleaded with the child and petitioned him, and offered more prayers.

At last the child grew weary of this amusement and turned toward home. The dog was praying at the time. He lay on his back and turned his eyes upon the retreating form.

Presently he struggled to his feet and started after the child. The latter wandered in a perfunctory way toward his home, stopping at times to investigate various matters. During one of these pauses he discovered the little dark-brown dog who was following him with the air of a footpad.

The child beat his pursuer with a small stick he had found. The dog lay down and prayed until the child had finished, and resumed his journey. Then he scrambled erect and took up the pursuit again.

On the way to his home the child turned many times and beat the dog, proclaiming with childish gestures that he held him in contempt as an unimportant dog, with no value save for a moment. For being this quality of animal the dog apologized and eloquently expressed regret, but he continued stealthily to follow the child. His manner grew so very guilty that he slunk like an assassin.

When the child reached his doorstep, the dog was industriously ambling a few yards in the rear. He became so agitated with shame when he again confronted the child that he forgot the dragging rope. He tripped upon it and fell forward.

The child sat down on the step and the two had another interview. During it the dog greatly exerted himself to please the child. He performed a few gambols with such abandon that the child suddenly saw him to be a valuable thing. He made a swift, avaricious charge and seized the rope.

He dragged his captive into a hall and up many long stairways in a dark tenement. The dog made willing efforts, but he could not hobble very skillfully up the stairs because he was very small and soft, and at last the pace of the engrossed child grew so energetic that the dog became panic-stricken. In his mind he was being dragged toward a grim unknown. His eyes grew wild with the terror of it. He began to wiggle his head frantically and to brace his legs.

The child redoubled his exertions. They had a battle on the stairs. The child was victorious because he was completely absorbed in his purpose, and because the dog was very small. He dragged his acquirement to the door of his home, and finally with triumph across the threshold.

No one was in. The child sat down on the floor and made overtures to the dog. These the dog instantly accepted. He beamed with affection upon his new friend. In a short time they were firm and abiding comrades.

When the child's family appeared, they made a great row. The dog was examined and commented upon and called names. Scorn was leveled at him from all eyes, so that he became much embarrassed and drooped like a scorched plant. But the child went sturdily to the center of the floor, and, at the top of his voice, championed the dog. It happened that he was roaring protestations, with his arms clasped about the dog's neck, when the father of the family came in from work.

The parent demanded to know what the blazes they were making the kid howl for. It was explained in many words that the infernal kid wanted to introduce a disreputable dog into the family.

A family council was held. On this depended the dog's fate, but he in no way heeded, being busily engaged in chewing the end of the child's dress.

The affair was quickly ended. The father of the family, it appears, was in a particularly savage temper that evening, and when he perceived that it would amaze and anger everybody if such a dog were allowed to remain, he decided that it should be so. The child, crying softly, took his friend off to a retired part of the room to hobnob with him, while the father quelled a fierce rebellion of his wife. So it came to pass that the dog was a member of the household.

He and the child were associated together at all times save when the child slept. The child became a guardian and a friend. If the large folk kicked the dog and threw things at him, the child made loud and violent objections. Once when the child had run, protesting loudly, with tears raining down his face and his arms outstretched, to protect his friend, he had been struck in the head with a very large saucepan from the hand of his father, enraged at some seeming lack of courtesy in the dog. Ever after, the family were careful how they threw things at the dog. Moreover, the latter grew very skilful in avoiding missiles and feet. In a small room containing a stove, a table, a bureau and some chairs, he would display strategic ability of a high order, dodging, feinting and scuttling about among the furniture. He could force three or four people armed with brooms, sticks and handfuls of coal, to use all their ingenuity to get in a blow. And even when they did, it was seldom that they could do him a serious injury or leave any imprint.

But when the child was present these scenes did not occur. It came to be recognized that if the dog was molested, the child would burst into sobs, and as the child, when started, was very riotous and practically unquenchable, the dog had therein a safeguard.

However, the child could not always be near. At night, when he was asleep, his dark-brown friend would raise from some black corner a wild, wailful cry, a song of infinite loneliness and despair, that would go shuddering and sobbing among the buildings of the block and cause people to swear. At these times the singer would often be chased all over the kitchen and hit with a great variety of articles.

Sometimes, too, the child himself used to beat the dog, although it is not known that he ever had what truly could be called a just cause. The dog always accepted these thrashings with an air of admitted guilt. He was too much of a dog to try to look to be a martyr or to plot revenge. He received the blows with deep humility, and furthermore he forgave his friend the moment the child had finished, and was ready to caress the child's hand with his little red tongue.

When misfortune came upon the child, and his troubles overwhelmed him, he would often crawl under the table and lay his small distressed head on the dog's back. The dog was ever sympathetic. It is not to be supposed that at such times he took occasion to refer to the unjust beatings his friend, when provoked, had administered to him.

He did not achieve any notable degree of intimacy with the other members of the family. He had no confidence in them, and the fear that he would express at their casual approach often exasperated them exceedingly. They used to gain a certain satisfaction in underfeeding him, but finally his friend the child grew to watch the matter with some care, and when he forgot, it, the dog was often successful in secret for himself.

So the dog prospered. He developed a large bark, which came wondrously from such a small rug of a

dog. He ceased to howl persistently at night. Sometimes, indeed, in his sleep, he would utter little yells,
as from pain, but that occurred, no doubt, when in
his dreams he encountered huge flaming dogs who
threatened him direfully.

His devotion to the child grew until it was a sub-
lime thing. He wagged at his approach; he sank
down in despair at his departure. He could detect
the sound of the child's step among all the noises of
the neighborhood. It was like a calling voice to him.

The scene of their companionship was a kingdom
governed by this terrible potentate, the child; but
neither criticism nor rebellion ever lived for an
instant in the heart of the one subject. Down in the
mystic, hidden fields of his little dog-soul bloomed
flowers of love and fidelity and perfect faith.

The child was in the habit of going on many expeditions to observe strange things in the vicinity. On
these occasions his friend usually jogged aimfully
along behind. Perhaps, though, he went ahead. This
necessitated his turning around every quarter-minute
to make sure the child was coming. He was filled
with a large idea of the importance of these journeys.
He would carry himself with such an air! He was
proud to be the retainer of so great a monarch.

One day, however, the father of the family got
quite exceptionally drunk. He came home and held
carnival with the cooking utensils, the furniture and

his wife. He was in the midst of this recreation when the child, followed by the dark-brown dog, entered the room. They were returning from their voyages.

The child's practiced eye instantly noted his father's state. He dived under the table, where experience had taught him was a rather safe place. The dog, lacking skill in such matters, was, of course, unaware of the true condition of affairs. He looked with interested eyes at his friend's sudden dive. He interpreted it to mean: Joyous gambol. He started to patter across the floor to join him. He was the picture of a little dark-brown dog en route to a friend.

The head of the family saw him at this moment. He gave a huge howl of joy, and knocked the dog down with a heavy coffee-pot. The dog, yelling in supreme astonishment and fear, writhed to his feet and ran for cover. The man kicked out with a ponderous foot. It caused the dog to swerve as if caught in a tide. A second blow of the coffee-pot laid him upon the floor.

Here, the child, uttering loud cries, came valiantly forth like a knight. The father of the family paid no attention to these calls of the child, but advanced with glee upon the dog. Upon being knocked down twice in swift succession, the latter apparently gave up all hope of escape. He rolled over on his back and held his paws in a peculiar manner. At the same time with his eyes and his ears he offered up a small prayer.

But the father was in a mood for having fun, and it occurred to him that it would be a fine thing to throw the dog out of the window. So he reached down and, grabbing the animal by a leg, lifted him, squirming, up. He swung him two or three times hilariously about his head, and then flung him with great accuracy through the window.

The soaring dog created a surprise in the block. A woman watering plants in an opposite window gave an involuntary shout and dropped a flower-pot. A man in another window leaned perilously out to watch the flight of the dog. A woman who had been hanging out clothes in a yard began to caper wildly. Her mouth was filled with clothes-pins, but her arms gave vent to a sort of exclamation. In appearance she was like a gagged prisoner. Children ran whooping.

The dark-brown body crashed in a heap on the roof of a shed five stories below. From thence it rolled to the pavement of an alleyway.

The child in the room far above burst into a long, dirge-like cry, and toddled hastily out of the room. It took him a long time to reach the alley, because his size compelled him to go downstairs backward, one step at a time, and holding with both hands to the step above.

When they came for him later, they found him seated, by the body of his dark-brown friend.

Memoirs of a Yellow Dog

[O. HENRY]

I don't suppose it will knock any of you people off your perch to read a contribution from an animal. Mr. Kipling and a good many others have demonstrated the fact that animals can express themselves in remunerative English, and no magazine goes to press nowadays without an animal story in it, except the old-style monthlies that are still running pictures of Bryan and the Mont Pelee horror.

But you needn't look for any stuck-up literature in my piece, such as Bearoo, the bear, and Snakoo, the snake, and Tammanoo, the tiger, talk in the jungle books. A yellow dog that's spent most of his life in a cheap New York flat, sleeping in a corner on an old sateen underskirt (the one she spilled port wine on at the Lady Longshoremen's banquet), mustn't be expected to perform any tricks with the art of speech.

I was born a yellow pup: date, locality, pedigree, and weight unknown. The first thing I can recollect, an old woman had me in a basket at Broadway and Twenty-third trying to sell me to a fat lady. Old Mother Hubbard was boosting me to beat the band as a genuine Pomeranian-Hambletonian-Red-Irish-Cochin-China-Stoke-Pogis fox terrier. The fat lady chased a V around among the samples of gros-grain flannelette in her shopping bag till she cornered it, and gave up. From that moment I was a pet—a mamma's own wootsey squidlums. Say, gentle reader, did you ever have a 200-pound woman breathing a flavor of Camembert cheese and Peau d'Espagne pick you up and wallop her nose all over you, remarking all the time in an Emma Eames tone of voice: "Oh, oo's um oodlum, doodlum, woodlum, toodlum, bitsy-witsy skoodlums?"

From a pedigreed yellow pup I grew up to be an anonymous yellow cur looking like a cross between an Angora cat and a box of lemons. But my mistress never tumbled. She thought that the two primeval pups that Noah chased into the ark were but a collateral branch of my ancestors. It took two policemen to keep her from entering me at the Madison Square Garden for the Siberian bloodhound prize.

I'll tell you about that flat. The house was the ordinary thing in New York, paved with Parian marble in the entrance hall and cobblestones above the first floor. Our flat was three—well, not flights—climbs up. My mistress rented it unfurnished, and put in the regular things—1903 antique upholstered parlor set, oil chromo of geishas in a Harlem tea house, rubber plant and husband.

By Sirius! there was a biped I felt sorry for. He was a little man with sandy hair and whiskers a good deal like mine. Henpecked?—well, toucans and flamingoes and pelicans all had their bills in him. He wiped the dishes and listened to my mistress tell about the cheap, ragged things the lady with the squirrel-skin coat on the second floor hung out on her line to dry. And every evening while she was getting supper she made him take me out on the end of a string for a walk.

If men knew how women pass the time when they are alone they'd never marry. Laura Lean Jibbey, peanut brittle, a little almond cream on the neck muscles, dishes unwashed, half an hour's talk with the iceman, reading a package of old letters, a couple of pickles and two bottles of malt extract, one hour peeking through a hole in the window shade into the flat across the air-shaft—that's about all there is to it. Twenty minutes before time for him to come home from work she straightens up the house, fixes her rat so it won't show, and gets out a lot of sewing for a ten-minute bluff.

I led a dog's life in that flat. 'Most all day I lay there in my corner watching that fat woman kill time. I slept sometimes and had pipe dreams about being out chasing cats into basements and growling at old ladies with black mittens, as a dog was intended to do. Then she would pounce upon me with a lot of that driveling poodle palaver and kiss me on the nose—but what could I do? A dog can't chew cloves.

I began to feel sorry for Hubby, dog my cats if I didn't. We looked so much alike that people noticed it when we went out; so we shook the streets that Morgan's cab drives down, and took to climbing the piles of last December's snow on the streets where cheap people live.

One evening when we were thus promenading, and I was trying to look like a prize St. Bernard, and the old man was trying to look like he wouldn't have murdered the first organ-grinder he heard play Mendelssohn's wedding-march, I looked up at him and said, in my way:

"What are you looking so sour about, you oakum trimmed lobster? She don't kiss you. You don't have to sit on her lap and listen to talk that would make the book of a musical comedy sound like the maxims of Epictetus. You ought to be thankful you're not a dog. Brace up, Benedick, and bid the blues begone."

The matrimonial mishap looked down at me with almost canine intelligence in his face.

"Why, doggie," says he, "good doggie. You almost look like you could speak. What is it, doggie—Cats?"

Cats! Could speak!

But, of course, he couldn't understand. Humans were denied the speech of animals. The only common ground of communication upon which dogs and men can get together is in fiction.

In the flat across the hall from us lived a lady with a black-and-tan terrier. Her husband strung it and took it out every evening, but he always came home cheerful and whistling. One day I touched noses with the black-and-tan in the hall, and I struck him for an elucidation.

"See, here, Wiggle-and-Skip," I says, "you know that it ain't the nature of a real man to play dry nurse to a dog in public. I never saw one leashed to a bow-wow yet that didn't look like he'd like to lick every other man that looked at him. But your boss comes in every day as perky and set up as an amateur prestidigitator doing the egg trick. How does he do it? Don't tell me he likes it."

"Him?" says the black-and-tan. "Why, he uses Nature's Own Remedy. He gets spifflicated. At first when we go out he's as shy as the man on the steamer who would rather play pedro when they make 'em all jackpots. By the time we've been in eight saloons he don't care whether the thing on the end of his line is a dog or a catfish. I've lost two inches of my tail trying to sidestep those swinging doors."

The pointer I got from that terrier—vaudeville please copy—set me to thinking.

One evening about six o'clock my mistress ordered him to get busy and do the ozone act for Lovey. I have concealed it until now, but that is what she called me. The black-and-tan was called "Tweetness." I consider that I have the bulge on him as far as you could chase a rabbit. Still "Lovey" is something of a nomenclatural tin can on the tail of one's self respect.

At a quiet place on a safe street I tightened the line of my custodian in front of an attractive, refined saloon. I made a dead-ahead scramble for the doors, whining like a dog in the press dispatches that lets the family know that little Alice is bogged while gathering lilies in the brook.

"Why, darn my eyes," says the old man, with a grin; "darn my eyes if the saffron-colored son of a seltzer lemonade ain't asking me in to take a drink. Lemme see—how long's it been since I saved shoe leather by keeping one foot on the footrest? I believe I'll—"

I knew I had him. Hot Scotches he took, sitting at a table. For an hour he kept the Campbells coming.

I sat by his side rapping for the waiter with my tail, and eating free lunch such as mamma in her flat never equaled with her homemade truck bought at a delicatessen store eight minutes before papa comes home.

When the products of Scotland were all exhausted except the rye bread the old man unwound me from the table leg and played me outside like a fisherman plays a salmon. Out there he took off my collar and threw it into the street.

"Poor doggie," says he; "good doggie. She shan't kiss you any more. 'S a darned shame. Good doggie, go away and get run over by a street car and be happy."

I refused to leave. I leaped and frisked around the old man's legs happy as a pug on a rug.

"You old flea-headed woodchuck-chaser," I said to him—"you moon-baying, rabbit-pointing, egg-stealing old beagle, can't you see that I don't want to leave you? Can't you see that we're both Pups in the Wood and the missis is the cruel uncle after you with the dish towel and me with the flea liniment and a pink bow to tie on my tail. Why not cut that all out and be pards forever more?"

Maybe you'll say he didn't understand—maybe he didn't. But he kind of got a grip on the Hot Scotches, and stood still for a minute, thinking.

"Doggie," says he, finally, "we don't live more than a dozen lives on this earth, and very few of us live to be more than 300. If I ever see that flat any more I'm a flat, and if you do you're flatter; and that's no flattery. I'm offering 60 to 1 that Westward Ho wins out by the length of a dachshund."

There was no string, but I frolicked along with my master to the Twenty-third Street ferry. And the cats on the route saw reason to give thanks that prehensile claws had been given them.

On the Jersey side my master said to a stranger who stood eating a currant bun:

"Me and my doggie, we are bound for the Rocky Mountains."

But what pleased me most was when my old man pulled both of my ears until I howled, and said:

"You common, monkey-headed, rat-tailed, sulphur-colored son of a doormat, do you know what I'm going to call you?"

I thought of "Lovey," and I whined dolefully.

"I'm going to call you 'Pete,'" says my master; and if I'd had five tails I couldn't have done enough wagging to do justice to the occasion.

The She-Wolf

[SAKI (H. H. MUNRO)]

Leonard Bilsiter was one of those people who
have failed to find this world attractive or
interesting, and who have sought compensa-
tion in an "unseen world" of their own experience
or imagination—or invention. Children do that sort
of thing successfully, but children are content to
convince themselves, and do not vulgarize their
beliefs by trying to convince other people. Leonard
Bilsiter's beliefs were for "the few," that is to say,
anyone who would listen to him.

His dabblings in the unseen might not have carried
him beyond the customary platitudes of the drawing-
room visionary if accident had not reinforced his
stock-in-trade of mystical lore. In company with a
friend, who was interested in a Ural mining concern,
he had made a trip across Eastern Europe at a moment

when the great Russian railway strike was developing from a threat to a reality; its outbreak caught him on the return journey, somewhere on the further side of Perm, and it was while waiting for a couple of days at a wayside station in a state of suspended locomotion that he made the acquaintance of a dealer in harness and metalware, who profitably whiled away the tedium of the long halt by initiating his English traveling companion in a fragmentary system of folklore that he had picked up from Trans-Baikal traders and natives. Leonard returned to his home circle garrulous about his Russian strike experiences, but oppressively reticent about certain dark mysteries, which he alluded to under the resounding title of Siberian Magic. The reticence wore off in a week or two under the influence of an entire lack of general curiosity, and Leonard began to make more detailed allusions to the enormous powers which this new esoteric force, to use his own description of it, conferred on the initiated few who knew how to wield it. His aunt, Cecilia Hoops, who loved sensation perhaps rather better than she loved the truth, gave him as clamorous an advertisement as anyone could wish for by retailing an account of how he had turned a vegetable marrow into a wood pigeon before her very eyes. As a manifestation of the possession of supernatural powers, the story was discounted in some quarters by the respect accorded to Mrs. Hoops' powers of imagination.

However divided opinion might be on the question of Leonard's status as a wonderworker or a charlatan, he certainly arrived at Mary Hampton's houseparty with a reputation for preeminence in one or other of those professions, and he was not disposed to shun such publicity as might fall to his share. Esoteric forces and unusual powers figured largely in whatever conversation he or his aunt had a share in, and his own performances, past and potential, were the subject of mysterious hints and dark avowals.

"I wish you would turn me into a wolf, Mr. Bilsiter," said his hostess at luncheon the day after his arrival.

"My dear Mary," said Colonel Hampton, "I never knew you had a craving in that direction."

"A she-wolf, of course," continued Mrs. Hampton, "it would be too confusing to change one's sex as well as one's species at a moment's notice."

"I don't think one should jest on these subjects," said Leonard.

"I'm not jesting, I'm quite serious, I assure you. Only don't do it today; we have only eight available bridge players, and it would break up one of our tables. Tomorrow we shall be a larger party. Tomorrow night, after dinner—"

"In our present imperfect understanding of these hidden forces I think one should approach them with humbleness rather than mockery," observed

Leonard, with such severity that the subject was forthwith dropped.

Clovis Sangrail had sat unusually silent during the discussion on the possibilities of Siberian Magic; after lunch he sidetracked Lord Pabham into the comparative seclusion of the billiard-room and delivered himself of a searching question.

"Have you such a thing as a she-wolf in your collection of wild animals? A she-wolf of moderately good temper?"

Lord Pabham considered. "There is Louisa," he said, "a rather fine specimen of the timber-wolf. I got her two years ago in exchange for some Arctic foxes. Most of my animals get to be fairly tame before they've been with me very long; I think I can say Louisa has an angelic temper, as she-wolves go. Why do you ask?"

"I was wondering whether you would lend her to me for tomorrow night," said Clovis, with the careless solicitude of one who borrows a collar stud or a tennis racquet.

"Tomorrow night?"

"Yes, wolves are nocturnal animals, so the late hours won't hurt her," said Clovis, with the air of one who has taken everything into consideration; "one of your men could bring her over from Pabham Park after dusk, and with a little help he ought to be able to smuggle her into the conservatory at the same moment that Mary Hampton makes an unobtrusive exit."

Lord Pabham stared at Clovis for a moment in pardonable bewilderment; then his face broke into a wrinkled network of laughter.

"Oh, that's your game, is it? You are going to do a little Siberian Magic on your own account. And is Mrs. Hampton willing to be a fellow-conspirator?"

"Mary is pledged to see me through with it, if you will guarantee Louisa's temper."

"I'll answer for Louisa," said Lord Pabham.

By the following day the houseparty had swollen to larger proportions, and Bilsiter's instinct for self-advertisement expanded duly under the stimulant of an increased audience. At dinner that evening he held forth at length on the subject of unseen forces and untested powers, and his flow of impressive eloquence continued unabated while coffee was being served in the drawing-room preparatory to a general migration to the card-room.

His aunt ensured a respectful hearing for his utterances, but her sensation-loving soul hankered after something more dramatic than mere vocal demonstration.

"Won't you do something to *convince* them of your powers, Leonard?" she pleaded; "change something into another shape. He can, you know, if he only chooses to," she informed the company.

"Oh, do," said Mavis Pellington earnestly, and her request was echoed by nearly everyone present. Even those who were not open to conviction were perfectly willing to be entertained by an exhibition of amateur conjuring.

Leonard felt that something tangible was expected of him.

"Has anyone present," he asked, "got a three-penny bit or some small object of no particular value—?"

"You're surely not going to make coins disappear, or something primitive of that sort?" said Clovis contemptuously.

"I think it very unkind of you not to carry out my suggestion of turning me into a wolf," said Mary Hampton, as she crossed over to the conservatory to give her macaws their usual tribute from the dessert dishes.

"I have already warned you of the danger of treating these powers in a mocking spirit," said Leonard solemnly.

"I don't believe you can do it," laughed Mary provocatively from the conservatory; "I dare you to do it if you can. I defy you to turn me into a wolf."

As she said this she was lost to view behind a clump of azaleas.

"Mrs. Hampton—" began Leonard with increased solemnity, but he got no further. A breath of chill air seemed to rush across the room, and at the same time the macaws broke forth into ear-splitting screams.

"What on earth is the matter with those confounded birds, Mary?" exclaimed Colonel Hampton; at the same moment an even more piercing scream from Mavis Pellington stampeded the entire company from their seats. In various attitudes of helpless horror or instinctive defense they confronted the evil-looking gray beast that was peering at them from amid a setting of fern and azalea.

Mrs. Hoops was the first to recover from the general chaos of fright and bewilderment.

"Leonard!" she screamed shrilly to her nephew, "turn it back into Mrs. Hampton at once! It may fly at us at any moment. Turn it back!"

"I—I don't know how to," faltered Leonard, who looked more scared and horrified than anyone.

"What!" shouted Colonel Hampton, "you've taken the abominable liberty of turning my wife into a wolf, and now you stand there calmly and say you can't turn her back again!"

To do strict justice to Leonard, calmness was not a distinguishing feature of his attitude at the moment.

"I assure you I didn't turn Mrs. Hampton into a wolf; nothing was farther from my intentions," he protested.

"Then where is she, and how came that animal into the conservatory?" demanded the Colonel.

"Of course we must accept your assurance that you didn't turn Mrs. Hampton into a wolf," said Clovis politely, "but you will agree that appearances are against you."

"Are we to have all these recriminations with that beast standing there ready to tear us to pieces?" wailed Mavis indignantly.

"Lord Pabham, you know a good deal about wild beasts—" suggested Colonel Hampton.

"The wild beasts that I have been accustomed to," said Lord Pabham, "have come with proper credentials from well-known dealers, or have been bred in my own menagerie. I've never before been confronted with an animal that walks unconcernedly out of an azalea bush, leaving a charming and popular hostess unaccounted for. As far as one can judge from *outward* characteristics," he continued, "it has the appearance of a well-grown female of the North American timber-wolf, a variety of the common species *Canis lupus.*"

"Oh, never mind its Latin name," screamed Mavis, as the beast came a step or two further into the room; "can't you entice it away with food, and shut it up where it can't do any harm?"

"If it is really Mrs. Hampton, who has just had a very good dinner, I don't suppose food will appeal to it very strongly," said Clovis.

"Leonard," beseeched Mrs. Hoops tearfully, "even if this is none of your doing can't you use your great powers to turn this dreadful beast into something harmless before it bites us all—a rabbit or something?"

"I don't suppose Colonel Hampton would care to have his wife turned into a succession of fancy animals as though we were playing a round game with her," interposed Clovis.

"I absolutely forbid it," thundered the Colonel.

"Most wolves that I've had anything to do with have been inordinately fond of sugar," said Lord Pabham; "if you like I'll try the effect on this one."

He took a piece of sugar from the saucer of his coffee cup and flung it to the expectant Louisa, who snapped it in midair. There was a sigh of relief from the company; a wolf that ate sugar when it might at the least have been employed in tearing macaws to pieces had already shed some of its terrors. The sigh deepened to a gasp of thanksgiving when Lord Pabham decoyed the animal out of the room by a pretended largesse of further sugar. There was an instant rush to the vacated conservatory. There was no trace of Mrs. Hampton except the plate containing the macaws' supper.

"The door is locked on the inside!" exclaimed Clovis, who had deftly turned the key as he affected to test it.

Everyone turned towards Bilsiter.

"If you haven't turned my wife into a wolf," said Colonel Hampton, "will you kindly explain where she has disappeared to, since she obviously could not have gone through a locked door? I will not press you for an explanation of how a North American timber-wolf suddenly appeared in the conservatory, but I think I have some right to inquire what has become of Mrs. Hampton."

Bilsiter's reiterated disclaimer was met with a general murmur of impatient disbelief.

"I refuse to stay another hour under this roof," declared Mavis Pellington.

"If our hostess has really vanished out of human form," said Mrs. Hoops, "none of the ladies of the party can very well remain. I absolutely decline to be chaperoned by a wolf!"

"It's a she-wolf," said Clovis soothingly.

The correct etiquette to be observed under the unusual circumstances received no further elucidation. The sudden entry of Mary Hampton deprived the discussion of its immediate interest.

"Some one has mesmerized me," she exclaimed crossly; "I found myself in the game larder, of all places, being fed with sugar by Lord Pabham. I hate being mesmerized, and the doctor has forbidden me to touch sugar."

The situation was explained to her, as far as it permitted of anything that could be called explanation.

"Then you *really* did turn me into a wolf, Mr. Bilsiter?" she exclaimed excitedly.

But Leonard had burned the boat in which he might now have embarked on a sea of glory. He could only shake his head feebly.

"It was I who took that liberty," said Clovis; "you see, I happen to have lived for a couple of years in northeastern Russia, and I have more than a tourist's acquaintance with the magic craft of that region. One does not care to speak about these strange powers, but once in a way, when one hears a lot of nonsense being talked about them, one is tempted to show what Siberian magic can accomplish in the hands of someone who really understands it. I yielded to that temptation. May I have some brandy? the effort has left me rather faint."

If Leonard Bilsiter could at that moment have transformed Clovis into a cockroach and then have stepped on him he would gladly have performed both operations.

Tito: The Story of the Coyote That Learned How

[**ERNEST THOMPSON SETON**]

I

Raindrop may deflect a thunderbolt, or a hair may ruin an empire, as surely as a spider-web once turned the history of Scotland; and if it had not been for one little pebble, this history of Tito might never have happened.

That pebble was lying on a trail in the Dakota Badlands, and one hot, dark night it lodged in the foot of a Horse that was ridden by a tipsy cowboy. The man got off, as a matter of habit, to know what was laming his Horse. But he left the reins on its neck instead of on the ground, and the Horse, taking advantage of this technicality, ran off in the darkness. Then the cowboy, realizing that he was afoot, lay down in a hollow under some buffalo-bushes and slept the loggish sleep of the befuddled.

The golden beams of the early summer sun were leaping from top to top of the wonderful Badland Buttes, when an old Coyote might have been seen trotting homeward along the Garner's Creek Trail with a Rabbit in her jaws to supply her family's breakfast.

Fierce war had for a long time been waged against the Coyote kind by the cattlemen of Billings County. Traps, guns, poison, and Hounds had reduced their number nearly to zero, and the few survivors had learned the bitter need of caution at every step. But the destructive ingenuity of man knew no bounds, and their numbers continued to dwindle.

The old Coyote quit the trail very soon, for nothing that man has made is friendly. She skirted along a low ridge, then across a little hollow where grew a few buffalo-bushes, and, after a careful sniff at a very stale human trail-scent, she crossed another near ridge on whose sunny side was the home of her brood. Again she cautiously circled, peered about, and sniffed, but, finding no sign of danger, went down to the doorway and uttered a low *woof-woof*. Out of the den, beside a sage-bush, there poured a procession of little Coyotes, merrily tumbling over one another. Then, barking little barks and growling little puppy growls, they fell upon the feast that their mother had brought, and gobbled and tussled while she looked on and enjoyed their joy.

Wolver Jake, the cowboy, had awakened from his chilly sleep about sunrise, in time to catch a glimpse of the Coyote passing over the ridge. As soon as she was out of sight he got on his feet and went to the edge, there to witness the interesting scene of the family breakfasting and frisking about within a few yards of him, utterly unconscious of any danger.

But the only appeal the scene had to him lay in the fact that the county had set a price on every one of these Coyotes' lives. So he got out his big .45 navy revolver, and notwithstanding his shaky condition, he managed somehow to get a sight on the mother as she was caressing one of the little ones that had finished its breakfast, and shot her dead on the spot.

The terrified cubs fled into the den, and Jake, failing to kill another with his revolver, came forward, blocked up the hole with stones, and leaving the seven little prisoners quaking at the far end, set off on foot for the nearest ranch, cursing his faithless Horse as he went.

In the afternoon he returned with his pard and tools for digging. The little ones had cowered all day in the darkened hole, wondering why their mother did not come to feed them, wondering at the darkness and the change. But late that day they heard sounds at the door. Then light was again let in. Some of the less cautious young ones ran forward to meet their mother, but their mother was not there—only two great rough brutes that began tearing open their home.

After an hour or more the diggers came to the end of the den, and here were the woolly, bright-eyed, little ones, all huddled in a pile at the farthest corner. Their innocent puppy faces and ways were not noticed by the huge enemy. One by one they were seized. A sharp blow, and each quivering, limp form was thrown into a sack to be carried to the nearest magistrate who was empowered to pay the bounties.

Even at this stage there was a certain individuality of character among the puppies. Some of them squealed and some of them growled when dragged out to die. One or two tried to bite. The one that had been slowest to comprehend the danger, had been the last to retreat, and so was on top of the pile, and therefore the first killed. The one that had first realized the peril had retreated first, and now crouched at the bottom of the pile. Coolly and remorselessly the others were killed one by one, and then this prudent little puppy was seen to be the last of the family. It lay perfectly still, even when touched, its eyes being half closed, as, guided by instinct, it tried to "play possum." One of the men picked it up. It neither squealed nor resisted. Then

Jake, realizing ever the importance of "standing in with the boss," said: "Say, let's keep that 'un for the children." So the last of the family was thrown alive into the same bag with its dead brothers, and, bruised and frightened, lay there very still, understanding nothing, knowing only that after a long time of great noise and cruel jolting it was again half strangled by a grip on its neck and dragged out, where were a lot of creatures like the diggers.

These were really the inhabitants of the Chimney-pot Ranch, whose brand is the Broad-arrow; and among them were the children for whom the cub had been brought. The boss had no difficulty in getting Jake to accept the dollar that the cub Coyote would have brought in bounty-money, and his present was turned over to the children. In answer to their question, "What is it?" a Mexican cow-hand present said it was a Coyotito—that is, a "little Coyote,"—and this, afterward shortened to "Tito," became the captive's name.

II

Tito was a pretty little creature, with woolly body, a puppy-like expression, and a head that was singularly broad between the ears.

But, as a children's pet, she—for it proved to be a female—was not a success. She was distant and distrustful. She ate her food and seemed healthy, but never responded to friendly advances; never even learned to come out of the box when called. This probably was due to the fact that the kindness of the small children was offset by the roughness of the men and boys, who did not hesitate to drag her out by the chain when they wished to see her. On these occasions she would suffer in silence, playing possum, shamming dead, for she seemed to know that that was the best thing to do. But as soon as released she would once more retire into the darkest corner of her box, and watch her tormentors with eyes that, at the proper angle, showed a telling glint of green.

Among the children of the ranchmen was a thirteen-year-old boy. The fact that he grew up to be like his father, a kind, strong, and thoughtful man, did not prevent him being, at this age, a shameless little brute.

Like all boys in that country, he practiced lasso-throwing, with a view to being a cowboy. Posts and stumps are uninteresting things to catch. His little brothers and sisters were under special protection of the Home Government. The Dogs ran far away whenever they saw him coming with the rope in his hands. So he must needs practice on the unfortunate Coyotito. She soon learned that her only hope for peace was to hide in the kennel, or, if thrown at when outside, to dodge the rope by lying as flat as possible on the ground. Thus Lincoln unwittingly taught the Coyote the dangers and limitations of a rope, and so he proved a blessing in disguise—a very perfect disguise. When the Coyote had thoroughly learned how to baffle the lasso, the boy terror devised a new amusement. He got a large trap of the kind known as "Fox-size." This he set in the dust as he had seen Jake set a Wolf-trap, close to the kennel, and over it he scattered scraps of meat, in the most approved style for Wolf-trapping. After a while Tito, drawn by the smell of the meat, came hungrily sneaking out toward it, and almost immediately was caught in the trap by one foot. The boy terror was watching from a near hiding-place. He gave a wild Indian whoop of delight, then rushed forward to drag the Coyote out of the box into which she had retreated. After some more delightful thrills of excitement and struggle he got his lasso on Tito's body, and, helped by a younger brother, a most promising pupil, he succeeded in setting the Coyote free from the trap before the grown-ups had discovered his amusement. One or two experiences like this taught her a mortal terror of traps. She soon learned the smell of the steel, and could detect and avoid it, no matter how cleverly Master Lincoln might bury it in the dust while the younger brother screened the operation from the intended victim by holding his coat over the door of Tito's kennel.

One day the fastening of her chain gave way, and Tito went off in an uncertain fashion, trailing her chain behind her. But she was seen by one of the men, who fired a charge of birdshot at her. The burning, stinging, and surprise of it all caused her to retreat to the one place she knew, her own kennel. The chain was fastened again, and Tito added to her ideas this, a horror of guns and the smell of gunpowder; and this also, that the one safety from them is to "lay low."

There were yet other rude experiences in store for the captive.

Poisoning Wolves was a topic of daily talk at the Ranch, so it was not surprising that Lincoln should privately experiment on Coyotito. The deadly strychnine was too well guarded to be available. So Lincoln hid some Rough on Rats in a piece of meat, threw it to the captive, and sat by to watch, as blithe and conscience-clear as any professor of chemistry trying a new combination.

Tito smelled the meat—everything had to be passed on by her nose. Her nose was in doubt. There was a good smell of meat, a familiar but unpleasant smell of human hands, and a strange new odor, but not the odor of the trap; so she bolted the morsel. Within a few minutes began to have fearful pains in stomach, followed by cramps. Now in all the Wolf tribe there is the instinctive habit to throw up anything that disagrees with them, and after a minute or two of suffering the Coyote sought relief in this way; and to make it doubly sure she hastily gobbled some blades of grass, and in less than an hour was quite well again.

Lincoln had put in poison enough for a dozen Coyotes. Had he put in less she could not have felt the pang till too late, but she recovered and never forgot that peculiar smell that means such awful after-pains. More than that, she was ready thenceforth to fly at once to the herbal cure that Nature had everywhere provided. An instinct of this kind grows quickly, once followed. It had taken minutes of suffering in the first place to drive her to the easement. Thenceforth, having learned, it was her first thought on feeling pain. The little miscreant did indeed succeed in having her swallow another bait with a small dose of poison, but she knew what to do now and had almost no suffering.

Later on, a relative sent Lincoln a Bull-terrier, and the new combination was a fresh source of spectacular interest for the boy, and of tribulation for the Coyote. It all emphasized for her that old idea to "lay low"—that is, to be quiet, unobtrusive, and hide when danger is in sight. The grown-ups of the household at length forbade these persecutions, and the Terrier was kept away from the little yard where the Coyote was chained up.

It must not be supposed that, in all this, Tito was a sweet, innocent victim. She had learned to bite. She had caught and killed several chickens by shamming sleep while they ventured to forage within the radius of her chain. And she had an inborn hankering to sing a morning and evening hymn, which procured for her many beatings. But she learned to shut up, the moment her opening notes were followed by a rattle of doors or windows, for these sounds of human nearness had frequently been followed by a *"bang"* and a charge of bird-shot, which somehow did no serious harm, though it severely stung her hide. And these experiences all helped to deepen her terror of guns and of those who used them. The object of these musical outpourings was not clear. They happened usually at dawn or dusk, but sometimes a loud noise at high noon would set her going. The song consisted of a volley of short barks, mixed with doleful squalls that never failed to set the Dogs astir in a responsive uproar, and once or twice had begotten a far-away answer from some wild Coyote in the hills.

There was one little trick that she had developed which was purely instinctive—that is, an inherited habit. In the back end of her kennel she had a little *cache* of bones, and knew exactly where one or two lumps of unsavory meat were buried within the radius of her chain, for a time of famine which never came. If anyone approached these hidden treasures she watched with anxious eyes, but made no other demonstration. If she saw that the meddler knew the exact place, she took an early opportunity to secrete them elsewhere.

After a year of this life Tito had grown to full size, and had learned many things that her wild kinsmen could not have learned without losing their lives in doing it. She knew and feared traps. She had learned to avoid poison baits, and knew what to do at once if, by some mistake, she should take one. She knew what guns are. She had learned to cut her morning and evening song very short. She had some acquaintance with Dogs, enough to make her hate and distrust them all. But, above all, she had this idea: whenever danger is near, the very best move possible is to lay low, be very quiet, do nothing to attract notice. Perhaps the little brain that looked out of those changing yellow eyes was the storehouse of much other knowledge about men, but what it was did not appear.

The Coyote was fully grown when the boss of the outfit bought a couple of thoroughbred Greyhounds, wonderful runners, to see whether he could not entirely extirpate the remnant of the Coyotes that still destroyed occasional Sheep and Calves on the range, and at the same time find amusement in the sport. He was tired of seeing that Coyote in the yard; so, deciding to use her for training the Dogs, he had her roughly thrown into a bag, then carried a quarter of a mile away and dumped out. At the same time the Greyhounds were slipped and chivvied on. Away they went bounding at their matchless pace, that nothing else on four legs could equal, and away went the Coyote, frightened by the noise of the men, frightened even to find herself free. Her quarter-mile start quickly shrank to one hundred yards, the one hundred to fifty, and on sped the flying Dogs. Clearly there was no chance for her. On and nearer they came. In another minute she would have been stretched out—not a doubt of it. But on a sudden she stopped, turned, and walked toward the Dogs with her tail serenely waving in the air and a friendly cock to her ears. Greyhounds are peculiar Dogs. Anything that runs away, they are going to catch and kill if they can. Anything that is calmly facing them becomes at once a non-combatant. They bounded over and past the Coyote before they could curb their own impetuosity, and returned completely nonplussed. Possibly they recognized the Coyote of the house-yard as she stood there wagging her tail. The ranchmen were nonplussed too. Every one was utterly taken aback, had a sense of failure, and the real victor in the situation was felt to be the audacious little Coyote.

The Greyhounds refused to attack an animal that wagged its tail and would not run; and the men, on seeing that the Coyote could *walk* far enough away to avoid being caught by hand, took their ropes (lassoes), and soon made her a prisoner once more. The next day they decided to try again, but this time they added the white Bull-terrier to the chasers. The Coyote did as before. The Greyhounds declined to be party to any attack on such a mild and friendly acquaintance. But the Bull-terrier, who came puffing and panting on the scene three minutes later, had no such scruples. He was not so tall, but he was heavier than the Coyote, and, seizing her by her wool-protected neck, he shook her till, in a surprisingly short time, she lay limp and lifeless, at which all the men seemed pleased, and congratulated the Terrier, while the Greyhounds pottered around in restless perplexity.

A stranger in the party, a newly arrived Englishman, asked if he might have the brush—the tail, he explained—and on being told to help himself, he picked up the victim by the tail, and with one awkward chop of his knife he cut it off at the middle, and the Coyote dropped, but gave a shrill yelp of pain. She was not dead, only playing possum, and now she leaped up and vanished into a near-by thicket of cactus and sage.

With Greyhounds a running animal is the signal for a run, so the two long-legged Dogs and the white broad-chested Dog dashed after the Coyote. But right across their path, by happy chance, there flashed a brown streak ridden by a snowy powder-puff, the visible but evanescent sign for Cottontail Rabbit. The Coyote was not in sight now. The Rabbit was, so the Greyhounds dashed after the Cottontail, who took advantage of a Prairie-dog's hole to seek safety in the bosom of Mother Earth, and the Coyote made good her escape.

She had been a good deal jarred by the rude treatment of the Terrier, and her mutilated tail gave her some pain. But otherwise she was all right, and she loped lightly away, keeping out of sight in the hollows, and so escaped among the fantastic buttes of the Badlands, to be eventually the founder of a new life among the Coyotes of the Little Missouri.

Moses was preserved by the Egyptians till he had outlived the dangerous period, and learned from them wisdom enough to be the savior of his people against those same Egyptians. So the bobtailed Coyote was not only saved by man and carried over the dangerous period of puppyhood: she was also unwittingly taught by him how to baffle the traps, poisons, lassoes, guns, and Dogs that had so long waged a war of extermination against her race.

III

Thus Tito escaped from man, and for the first time found herself face to face with the whole problem of life; for now she had her own living to get.

A wild animal has three sources of wisdom:

First, *the experience of its ancestors,* in the form of instinct, which is inborn learning, hammered into the race by ages of selection and tribulation. This is the most important to begin with, because it guards him from the moment he is born.

Second, *the experience of his parents and comrades,* learned chiefly by example. This becomes most important as soon as the young can run.

Third, *the personal experience of the animal itself.* This grows in importance as the animal ages.

The weakness of the first is its fixity; it cannot change to meet quickly changing conditions. The weakness of the second is the animal's inability freely to exchange ideas by language. The weakness of the third is the danger in acquiring it. But the three together are a strong arch.

Now, Tito was in a new case. Perhaps never before had a Coyote faced life with unusual advantages in the third kind of knowledge, none at all in the second, and with the first dormant. She traveled rapidly away from the ranchmen, keeping out of sight, and sitting down once in a while to lick her wounded tail-stump. She came at last to a Prairie-dog town. Many of the inhabitants were out, and they barked at the intruder, but all dodged down as soon as she came near. Her instinct taught her to try and catch one, but she ran about in vain for some time, and then gave it up. She would have gone hungry that night but that she found a couple of Mice in the long grass by the river. Her mother had not taught her to hunt, but her instinct did, and the accident that she had an unusual brain made her profit very quickly by her experience.

In the days that followed she quickly learned how to make a living; for Mice, Ground Squirrels, Prairie-dogs, Rabbits, and Lizards were abundant, and many of these could be captured in open chase. But open chase, and sneaking as near as possible before beginning the open chase, lead naturally to stalking for a final spring. And before the moon had changed the Coyote had learned how to make a comfortable living.

Once or twice she saw the men with the Grey-hounds coming her way. Most Coyotes would, per-haps, have barked in bravado, or would have gone up to some high place whence they could watch the enemy; but Tito did no such foolish thing. Had she run, her moving form would have caught the eyes of the Dogs, and then nothing could have saved her. She dropped where she was, and lay flat until the danger had passed. Thus her ranch training to lay low began to stand her in good stead, and so it came about that her weakness was her strength. The Coyote kind had so long been famous for their speed, had so long learned to trust in their legs, that they never dreamed of a creature that could run them down. They were accustomed to play with their pursuers, and so rarely bestirred themselves to run from Greyhounds, till it was too late. But Tito, brought up at the end of a chain, was a poor runner. She had no reason to trust her legs. She rather trusted her wits, and so lived.

During that summer she stayed about the Little Missouri, learning the tricks of small-game hunting that she should have learned before she shed her milk-teeth, and gaining in strength and speed. She kept far away from all the ranches, and always hid on seeing a man or a strange beast, and so passed the summer alone. During the daytime she was not lonely, but when the sun went down she would feel the impulse to sing that wild song of the West which means so much to the Coyotes. It is not the invention of an individual nor of the present, but was slowly built out of the feelings of all Coyotes in all ages. It expresses their nature and the Plains that made their nature. When one begins it, it takes hold of the rest, as the fife and drum do with soldiers, or the *ki-yi* war-song with Indian braves. They respond to it as a bell-glass does to a certain note the moment that note is struck, ignoring other sounds. So the Coyote, no matter how brought up, must vibrate at the night song of the Plains, for it touches something in himself.

They sing it after sundown, when it becomes the rallying cry of their race and the friendly call to a neighbor; and, they sing it as one boy in the woods holloas to another to say, "All's well! Here am I. Where are you?" A form of it they sing to the rising moon, for this is the time for good hunting to begin. They sing when they see the new camp-fire, for the same reason that a Dog barks at a stranger. Yet another weird chant they have for the dawning before they steal quietly away from the offing of the camp—a wild, weird, squalling refrain: *Wow-wow-wow-wow-wow-w-o-o-o-o-o-o-w,* again and again; and doubtless with many another change that man cannot distinguish any more than the Coyote can distinguish the words in the cowboy's anathemas.

Tito instinctively uttered her music at the proper times. But sad experiences had taught her to cut it short and keep it low. Once or twice she had got a far-away reply from one of her own race, whereupon she had quickly ceased and timidly quit the neighborhood.

One day, when on the Upper Garner's Creek, she found the trail where a piece of meat had been dragged along. It was a singularly inviting odor, and she followed it, partly out of curiosity. Presently she came on a piece of the meat itself. She was hungry; she was always hungry now. It was tempting, and although it had a peculiar odor, she swallowed it. Within a few minutes she felt a terrific pain. The memory of the poisoned meat the boy had given her, was fresh. With trembling, foaming jaws she seized some blades of grass, and her stomach threw off the meat; but she fell in convulsions on the ground.

The trail of meat dragged along and the poison baits had been laid the day before by Wolfer Jake. This morning he was riding the drag, and on coming up from the draw he saw, far ahead, the Coyote struggling. He knew, of course, that it was poisoned, and rode quickly up; but the convulsions passed as he neared. By a mighty effort, at the sound of the Horse's hoofs the Coyote arose to her front feet. Jake drew his revolver and fired, but the only effect was fully to alarm her. She tried to run, but her hind legs were paralyzed. She put forth all her strength, dragging her hind legs. Now, when the poison was no longer in the stomach, willpower could do a great deal. Had she been allowed to lie down then she would have been dead in five minutes; but the revolver shots and the man coming stirred her to strenuous action. Madly she struggled again and again to get her hind legs to work. All the force of desperate intent she brought to bear. It was like putting forth tenfold power to force the nervous fluids through their blocked-up channels as she dragged herself with marvelous speed downhill. What is nerve but will? The dead wires of her legs were hot with this fresh power, multiplied, injected, blasted into them. They had to give in. She felt them thrill with life again. Each wild shot from the gun lent vital help. Another fierce attempt, and one hind leg obeyed the call to duty. A few more bounds, and the other, too, fell in. Then lightly she loped away among the broken buttes, defying the agonizing gripe that still kept on inside.

Had Jake held off then she would yet have laid down and died; but he followed and fired and fired, till in another mile she bounded free from pain, saved from her enemy by himself. He had compelled her to take the only cure, so she escaped.

And these were the ideas that she harvested that day: That curious smell on the meat stands for mortal agony. Let it alone! And she never forgot it; thenceforth she knew strychnine.

Fortunately, Dogs, traps, and strychnine do not wage war at once, for the Dogs are as apt to be caught or poisoned as the Coyotes. Had there been a single Dog in the hunt that day Tito's history would have ended.

IV

When the weather grew cooler toward the end of Autumn Tito had gone far toward repairing the defects in her early training. She was more like an ordinary Coyote in her habits now, and she was more disposed to sing the sundown song. One night, when she got a response, she yielded to the impulse again to call, and soon afterward a large, dark Coyote appeared. The fact that he was there at all was a guarantee of unusual gifts, for the war against his race was waged relentlessly by the cattlemen. He approached with caution. Tito's mane bristled with mixed feelings at the sight of one of her own kind. She crouched flat on the ground and waited. The newcomer came stiffly forward, nosing the wind; then up the wind nearly to her. Then he walked around so that she should wind him, and raising his tail, gently waved it. The first acts meant armed neutrality, but the last was a distinctly friendly signal. Then he approached and she rose up suddenly and stood as high as she could to be smelled. Then she wagged the stump of her tail, and they considered themselves acquainted.

The newcomer was a very large Coyote, half as tall again as Tito, and the dark patch on his shoulders was so large and black that the cow-boys when they came to know him, called him Saddleback. From that time these two continued more or less together. They were not always close together, often were miles apart during the day, but toward night one or the other would get on some high open place and sing the loud

Yap-yap-yap-yow-wow-wow-wow-wow,

and they would forgather for some foray on hand.

The physical advantages were with Saddleback, but the greater cunning was Tito's, so that she in time became the leader. Before a month a third Coyote had appeared on the scene and become also a member of this loose-bound fraternity, and later two more appeared. Nothing succeeds like success. The little bobtailed Coyote had had rare advantages of training just where the others were lacking: she knew the devices of man. She could not tell about these in words, but she could by the aid of a few signs and a great deal of example. It soon became evident that her methods of hunting were successful, whereas, when they went without her, they often had hard luck. A man at Boxelder Ranch had twenty Sheep. The rules of the county did not allow anyone to own more, as this was a Cattle-range. The Sheep were guarded by a large and fierce Collie. One day in winter two of the Coyotes tried to raid this flock by a bold dash, and all they got was a mauling from the Collie. A few days later the band returned at dusk. Just how Tito arranged it, man cannot tell. We can only guess how she taught them their parts, but we know that she surely did. The Coyotes hid in the willows. Then Saddleback, the bold and swift, walked openly toward the Sheep and barked a loud defiance. The Collie jumped up with bristling mane and furious growl, then, seeing the foe, dashed straight at him. Now was the time for the steady nerve and the unfailing limbs. Saddleback let the Dog come near enough *almost* to catch him, and so beguiled him far and away into the woods, while the other Coyotes, led by Tito, stampeded the Sheep in twenty directions; then following the farthest, they killed several and left them in the snow. In the gloom of descending night the Dog and his master labored till they had gathered the bleating survivors; but next morning they found that four had been driven far away and killed, and the Coyotes had had a banquet royal.

The shepherd poisoned the carcasses and left them. Next night the Coyotes returned. Tito sniffed the now frozen meat, detected the poison, gave a warning growl, and scattered filth over the meat, so that none of the band should touch it. One, however, who was fast and foolish, persisted in feeding in spite of Tito's warning, and when they came away he was lying poisoned and dead in the snow.

V

Jake now heard on all sides that the Coyotes were getting worse. So he set to work with many traps and much poison to destroy those on the Garner's Creek, and every little while he would go with the Hounds and scour the Little Missouri south and east of the Chimney-pot Ranch; for it was understood that he must never run the Dogs in country where traps and poison were laid. He worked in his erratic way all winter, and certainly did have some success. He killed a couple of Grey Wolves, said to be the last of their race, and several Coyotes, some of which, no doubt, were of the Bobtailed pack, which thereby lost those members which were lacking in wisdom.

Yet that winter was marked by a series of Coyote raids and exploits; and usually the track in the snow or the testimony of eye-witnesses told that the master spirit of it all was a little Bobtailed Coyote.

One of these adventures was the cause of much talk. The Coyote challenge sounded close to the Chimney-pot Ranch after sundown. A dozen Dogs responded with the usual clamor. But only the Bull-terrier dashed away toward the place whence the Coyotes had called, for the reason that he only was loose. His chase was fruitless, and he came back growling. Twenty minutes later there was another Coyote yell close at hand. Off dashed the Terrier as

before. In a minute his excited yapping told that he
had sighted his game and was in full chase. Away he
went, furiously barking, until his voice was lost afar,
and nevermore was heard. In the morning the men
read in the snow the tale of the night. The first cry
of the Coyotes was to find out if all the Dogs were
loose; then, having found that only one was free, they
laid a plan. Five Coyotes hid along the side of the
trail; one went forward and called till it had decoyed
the rash Terrier, and then led him right into the
ambush. What chance had he with six? They tore
him limb from limb, and devoured him, too, at the
very spot where once he had worried Coyotito. And
next morning, when the men came, they saw by the
signs that the whole thing had been planned, and
that the leader whose cunning had made it a success
was a little Bob-tailed Coyote.

The men were angry, and Lincoln was furious; but
Jake remarked: "Well, I guess that Bobtail came back
and got even with that Terrier."

VI

When spring was near, the annual love-season of the
Coyotes came on. Saddleback and Tito had been
together merely as companions all winter, but now a
new feeling was born. There was not much courting. Saddleback simply showed his teeth to possible

rivals. There was no ceremony. They had been friends for months, and now, in the light of the new feeling, they naturally took to each other and were mated. Coyotes do not give each other names as do mankind, but have one sound like a growl and short howl, which stands for "mate" or "husband" or "wife." This they use in calling to each other, and it is by recognizing the tone of the voice that they know who is calling.

The loose rambling brotherhood of the Coyotes was broken up now, for the others also paired off, and since the returning warm weather was bringing out the Prairie-dogs and small game, there was less need to combine for hunting. Ordinarily Coyotes do not sleep in dens or in any fixed place. They move about all night while it is cool, then during the daytime they get a few hours' sleep in the sun, on some quiet hillside that also gives a chance to watch out. But the mating season changes this habit somewhat.

As the weather grew warm Tito and Saddleback set about preparing a den for the expected family. In a warm little hollow, an old Badger abode was cleaned out, enlarged, and deepened. A quantity of leaves and grass was carried into it and arranged in a comfortable nest. The place selected for it was a dry sunny nook among the hills, half a mile west of the Little Missouri. Thirty yards from it was a ridge which commanded a wide view of the grassy slopes and cottonwood groves by the river. Men would have called the spot very beautiful, but it is tolerably certain that that side of it never touched the Coyotes at all.

Tito began to be much preoccupied with her impending duties. She stayed quietly in the neighborhood of the den, and lived on such food as Saddleback brought her, or she herself could easily catch, and also on the little stores that she had buried at other times. She knew every Prairie-dog town in the region, as well as all the best places for Mice and Rabbits.

Not far from the den was the very Dog-town that first she had crossed, the day she had gained her liberty and lost her tail. If she were capable of such retrospect, she must have laughed to herself to think what a fool she was then. The change in her methods was now shown. Somewhat removed from the others, a Prairie-dog had made his den in the most approved style, and now when Tito peered over he was feeding on the grass ten yards from his own door. A Prairie-dog away from the others is, of course, easier to catch than one in the middle of the town, for he has but one pair of eyes to guard him; so Tito set about stalking this one. How was she to do it when there was no cover, nothing but short grass and a few low weeds? The White-bear knows how to approach the Seal on the flat ice, and the

Indian how to get within striking distance of the grazing Deer. Tito knew how to do the same trick, and although one of the town Owls flew over with a warning chuckle, Tito set about her plan. A Prairie-dog cannot see well unless he is sitting up on his hind legs; his eyes are of little use when he is nosing in the grass; and Tito knew this. Further, a yellowish-gray animal on a yellowish-gray landscape is invisible till it moves. Tito seemed to know that. So, without any attempt to crawl or hide, she walked gently up-wind toward the Prairie-dog. Upwind, not in order to prevent the Prairie-dog smelling her, but so that she could smell him, which came to the same thing. As soon as the Prairie-dog sat up with some food in his hand she froze into a statue. As soon as he dropped again to nose in the grass, she walked steadily nearer, watching his every move so that she might be motionless each time he sat up to see what his distant brothers were barking at. Once or twice he seemed alarmed by the calls of his friends, but he saw nothing and resumed his feeding. She soon cut the fifty yards down to ten, and the ten to five, and still was undiscovered. Then, when again the Prairie-dog dropped down to seek more fodder, she made a quick dash, and bore him off kicking and squealing. Thus does the angel of the pruning-knife lop off those that are heedless and foolishly indifferent to the advantages of society.

VII

Tito had many adventures in which she did not come out so well. Once she nearly caught an Antelope fawn, but the hunt was spoiled by the sudden appearance of the mother, who gave Tito a stinging blow on the side of the head and ended her hunt for that day. She never again made that mistake—she had sense. Once or twice she had to jump to escape the strike of a Rattlesnake. Several times she had been fired at by hunters with long-range rifles. And more and more she had to look out for the terrible Grey Wolves. The Grey Wolf, of course, is much larger and stronger than the Coyote, but the Coyote has the advantage of speed, and can always escape in the open. All it must beware of is being caught in a corner. Usually when a Grey Wolf howls the Coyotes go quietly about their business elsewhere.

Tito had a curious fad, occasionally seen among the Wolves and Coyotes, of carrying in her mouth, for miles, such things as seemed to be interesting and yet were not tempting as eatables. Many a time had she trotted a mile or two with an old Buffalo-horn or a cast-off shoe, only to drop it when something else attracted her attention. The cow-boys who remark these things have various odd explanations to offer: one, that it is done to stretch the jaws, or keep them in practice, just as a man in training carries weights. Coyotes have, in common with Dogs and Wolves, the habit of calling at certain stations along their line of travel, to leave a record of their visit. These stations may be a stone, a tree, a post, or an old Buffalo-skull, and the Coyote calling there can learn, by the odor and track of the last comer, just who the caller was, whence he came, and whither he went. The whole country is marked out by these intelligence depots. Now it often happens that a Coyote, that has not much else to do will carry a dry bone or some other useless object in its mouth, but sighting the signal-post, will go toward it to get the news, lay down the bone, and afterwards forget to take it along, so that the signal-posts in time become further marked with a curious collection of odds and ends.

This singular habit was the cause of a disaster to the Chimney-pot Wolf-hounds, and a corresponding advantage to the Coyotes in the war. Jake had laid a line of poison baits on the western bluffs. Tito knew what they were, and spurned them as usual; but finding more later, she gathered up three or four and crossed the Little Missouri toward the ranch-house. This she circled at a safe distance; but when something made the pack of Dogs break out into clamor, Tito dropped the baits, and next day, when the Dogs were taken out for exercise they found and devoured these scraps of meat, so that in ten minutes, there were four hundred dollars' worth of Grey-hounds lying dead. This led to an edict against poisoning in that district, and thus was a great boon to the Coyotes.

Tito quickly learned that not only each kind of game must be hunted in a special way, but also different ones of each kind may require quite different treatment. The Prairie-dog with the outlying den was really an easy prey, but the town was quite compact now that he was gone. Near the center of it was a fine, big, fat Prairie-dog, a perfect alderman, that she had made several vain attempts to capture. On one occasion she had crawled almost within leaping distance, when the angry *bizz* of a Rattlesnake just ahead warned her that she was in danger. Not that the Rattler cared anything about the Prairie-dog, but he did not wish to be disturbed; and Tito, who had an instinctive fear of the Snake, was forced to abandon the hunt. The open stalk proved an utter failure with the Alderman, for the situation of his den made every Dog in the town his sentinel; but he was too good to lose, and Tito waited until circumstances made a new plan.

All Coyotes have a trick of watching from a high look-out whatever passes along the roads. After it has passed they go down and examine its track. Tito had this habit, except that she was always careful to keep out of sight herself.

One day a wagon passed from the town to the southward. Tito lay low and watched it. Something dropped on the road. When the wagon was out of sight Tito sneaked down, first to smell the trail as a matter of habit, second to see what it was that had dropped. The object was really an apple, but Tito saw only an unattractive round green thing like a cactus-leaf without spines, and of a peculiar smell. She snuffed it, spurned it, and was about to pass on; but the sun shone on it so brightly, and it rolled so curiously when she pawed, that she picked it up in a mechanical way and trotted back over the rise, where are found herself at the Dog-town. Just then two great Prairie-hawks came skimming like pirates over the plain. As soon as they were in sight the Prairie-dogs all barked, jerking their tails at each bark, and hid below. When all were gone Tito walked on toward the hole of the big fat fellow whose body she coveted, and dropping the apple on the ground a couple of feet from the rim of the crater that formed his home, she put her nose down to enjoy the delicious smell of Dog-fat. Even his den smelled more fragrant than those of the rest. Then she went quietly behind a greasewood bush, in a lower place some twenty yards away, and lay flat. After a few seconds some venturesome Prairie-dog looked out, and seeing nothing, gave the "all's well" bark. One by one they came out, and in twenty minutes the town was alive as before. One of the last to come out was the fat old Alderman. He always took good care of his own precious self. He peered out cautiously a few times, then climbed to the top of his look-out. A Prairie-dog hole is shaped like a funnel, going straight down. Around the top of this is built a high ridge which serves as a look-out, and also makes sure that, no matter how they may slip in their hurry, they are certain to drop into the funnel and be swallowed up by the all-protecting earth. On the outside the ground slopes away gently from the funnel. Now, when the Alderman saw that strange round thing at his threshold he was afraid. Second inspection led him to believe that it was not dangerous, but was probably interesting. He went cautiously toward it, smelled it, and tried to nibble it; but the apple rolled away, for it was round, and the ground was smooth as well as sloping. The Prairie-dog followed and gave it a nip which satisfied him that the strange object would make good eating. But each time he nibbled, it rolled farther away. The coast seemed clear, all the other Prairie-dogs were out, so the fat Alderman did not hesitate to follow up the dodging, shifting apple.

This way and that it wriggled, and he followed. Of course it worked toward the low place where grew the greasewood bush. The little tastes of apple that he got only whetted his appetite. The Alderman was more and more interested. Foot by foot he was led from his hole toward that old, familiar bush and had no thought of anything but the joy of eating. And Tito curled herself and braced her sinewy legs, and measured the distance between, until it dwindled to not more than three good jumps; then up and like an arrow she went, and grabbed and bore him off at last.

It will never be known whether it was accident or design that led to the placing of that apple, but it proved important, and if such a thing were to happen once or twice to a smart Coyote,—and it is usually clever ones that get such chances,—it might easily grow into a new trick of hunting.

After a hearty meal Tito buried the rest in a cold place, not to get rid of it, but to hide it for future use; and a little later, when she was too weak to hunt much, her various hoards of this sort came in very useful. True, the meat had turned very strong; but Tito was not critical, and she had no fears or theories of microbes, so suffered no ill effects.

VIII

The lovely Hiawathan spring was touching all things in the fairy Badlands. Oh, why are they called Badlands? If Nature sat down deliberately on the eighth day of creation and said, "Now work is done, let's play; let's make a place that shall combine everything that is finished and wonderful and beautiful—a paradise for man and bird and beast," it was surely then that she made these wild, fantastic hills, teeming with life, radiant with gayest flowers, varied with sylvan groves, bright with prairie sweeps and brimming lakes and streams. In foreground, offing, and distant hills that change at every step, we find some proof that Nature squandered here the riches that in other lands she used as sparingly as gold, with colorful sky above and colorful land below, and the distance blocked by sculptured buttes that are built of precious stones and ores, and tinged as by a lasting and unspeakable sunset. And yet, for all this ten tunes gorgeous wonderland enchanted, blind man has found no better name than one which says, *the road to it is hard.*

The little hollow west of Chimney Butte was freshly grassed. The dangerous-looking Spanish bayonets, that through the bygone winter had waged war with all things, now sent out their contribution to the peaceful triumph of the spring, in flowers that have stirred even the chilly scientists to name them *Gloriosa;* and the cactus, poisonous, most reptilian of herbs, surprised the world with a splendid bloom as little like itself as the pearl is like its mother shellfish. The sage and the greasewood lent their gold, and the sand-anemone tinged the Badland hills like bluish snow; and in the air and earth and hills on every hand was felt the fecund promise of the spring. This was the end of the winter famine, the beginning of the summer feast, and this was the time by the All-mother, ordained when first the little Coyotes should see the light of day.

A mother does not have to learn to love her help-less, squirming brood. They bring the love with them—not much or little, not measurable, but per-fect love. And in that dimly lighted warm abode she fondled them and licked them and cuddled them with heartful warmth of tenderness, that was as much a new epoch in her life as in theirs.

But the pleasure of loving them was measured in the same measure as anxiety for their safety. In bygone days her care had been mainly for herself. All she had learned in her strange puppyhood, all she had picked up since, was bent to the main idea of self-preservation. Now she was ousted from her own affections by her brood. Her chief care was to keep their home concealed, and this was not very hard at first, for she left them only when she must, to supply her own wants.

She came and went with great care, and only after spying well the land so that none should see and find the place of her treasure. If it were possible for the little ones' idea of their mother and the cowboys' idea to be set side by side they would be found to have nothing in common, though both were right in their point of view. The ranchmen knew the Coyote

only as a pair of despicable, cruel jaws, borne around
on tireless legs, steered by incredible cunning, and
leaving behind a track of destruction. The little ones
knew her as a loving, gentle, all-powerful guardian.
For them her breast was soft and warm and infinitely
tender. She fed and warmed them, she was their wise
and watchful keeper. She was always at hand with
food when they hungered, with wisdom to foil the
cunning of their foes, and with a heart of courage
tried to crown her well-laid plans for them with
uniform success.

A baby Coyote is a shapeless, senseless, wriggling,
and—to every one but its mother—a most uninteresting little lump. But after its eyes are open, after it
has developed its legs, after it has learned to play in
the sun with its brothers, or run at the gentle call of
its mother when she brings home game for it to feed
on, the baby Coyote becomes one of the cutest,
dearest little rascals on earth. And when the nine that
made up Coyotito's brood had reached this stage, it
did not require the glamour of motherhood to make
them objects of the greatest interest.

The summer was now on. The little ones were
beginning to eat flesh-meat, and Tito, with some
assistance from Saddleback, was kept busy to supply
both themselves and the brood. Sometimes she
brought them a Prairie-dog, at other times she
would come home with a whole bunch of Gophers

and Mice in her jaws; and once or twice, by the clever trick of relay-chasing, she succeeded in getting one of the big Northern Jack-rabbits for the little folks at home.

After they had feasted they would lie around in the sun for a time. Tito would mount guard on a bank and scan the earth and air with her keen, brassy eye, lest any dangerous foe should find their happy valley; and the merry pups played little games of tag, or chased the Butterflies, or had apparently desperate encounters with each other, or tore and worried the bones and feathers that now lay about the threshold of the home. One, the least, for there is usually a runt, stayed near the mother and climbed on her back or pulled at her tail. They made a lovely picture as they played, and the wrestling group in the middle seemed the focus of it all at first; but a keener, later look would have rested on the mother, quiet, watchful, not without anxiety, but, above all, with a face full of motherly tenderness. Oh, she was so proud and happy, and she would sit there and watch them and silently love them till it was time to go home, or until some sign of distant danger showed. Then, with a low growl, she gave the signal, and all disappeared from sight in a twinkling, after which she would set off to meet and turn the danger, or go on a fresh hunt for food.

IX

Oliver Jake had several plans for making a fortune, but each in turn was abandoned as soon as he found that it meant work. At one time or other most men of this kind see the chance of their lives in a poultry-farm. They cherish the idea that somehow the poultry do all the work. And without troubling himself about the details, Jake devoted an unexpected windfall to the purchase of a dozen Turkeys for his latest scheme. The Turkeys were duly housed in one end of Jake's shanty, so as to be well guarded, and for a couple of days were the object of absorbing interest, and had the best of care—too much, really. But Jake's ardor waned about the third day; then the recurrent necessity for long celebrations at Medora, and the ancient allurements of idle hours spent lying on the tops of sunny buttes and of days spent sponging on the hospitality of distant ranches, swept away the last pretence of attention to his poultry-farm. The Turkeys were utterly neglected—left to forage for themselves; and each time that Jake returned to his uninviting shanty, after a few days' absence, he found fewer birds, till at last none but the old Gobbler was left.

Jake cared little about the loss, but was filled with indignation against the thief.

He was now installed as wolver to the Broadarrow outfit. That is, he was supplied with poison, traps, and Horses, and was also entitled to all he could make out of Wolf bounties. A reliable man would have gotten pay in addition, for the ranchmen are generous, but Jake was not reliable.

Every wolver knows, of course, that his business naturally drops into several well-marked periods.

In the late winter and early spring—the love-season —the Hounds will not hunt a She-wolf. They will quit the trail of a He-wolf at this time—to take up that of a She-wolf, but when they do overtake her, they, for some sentimental reason, invariably let her go in peace. In August and September the young Coyotes and Wolves are just beginning to run alone, and they are then easily trapped and poisoned. A month or so later the survivors have learned how to take care of themselves, but in the early summer the wolver knows that there are dens full of little ones all through the hills. Each den has from five to fifteen pups, and the only difficulty is to know the whereabouts of these family homes.

One way of finding the dens is to watch from some tall butte for a Coyote carrying food to its brood. As this kind of wolving involved much lying still, it suited Jake very well. So, equipped with a Broadarrow Horse and the boss's field-glasses, he put in week after week at den-hunting—that is, lying asleep in some possible look-out, with an occasional glance over the country when it seemed easier to do that than to lie still.

The Coyotes had learned to avoid the open. They generally went homeward along the sheltered hollows; but this was not always possible, and one day, while exercising his arduous profession in the country west of Chimney Butte, Jake's glasses and glance fell by chance on a dark spot which moved along an open hillside. It was gray, and . . . even Jake knew that that meant Coyote. If it had been a gray Wolf it would have been with tail up. A Fox would have had the large ears and tail and the yellow color would have marked it. . . . That dark shade from the front end meant something in his mouth—probably something being carried home—and that would mean a den of little ones.

He made careful note of the place, and returned there next day to watch, selecting a high butte near where he had seen the Coyote carrying the food. But all day passed, and he saw nothing. Next day, however, he descried a dark Coyote, old Saddleback, carrying a large Bird, and by the help of the glasses he made out that it was a Turkey, and then he knew that the yard at home was quite empty, and he also knew where the rest of them had gone, and vowed terrible vengeance when he should find the den. He followed Saddleback with his eyes as far as possible, and that was no great way, then went to the place to see if he could track him any farther; but he found no guiding signs, and he did not chance on the little hollow the was the playground of Tito's brood.

Meanwhile Saddleback came to the little hollow and gave the low call that always conjured from the earth the unruly procession of the nine riotous little pups, and they dashed at the Turkey and pulled and worried till it was torn up, and each that got a piece ran to one side alone and silently proceeded to eat, seizing his portion in his jaws when another came near, and growling his tiny growl as he showed the brownish whites of his eyes in his effort to watch the intruder. Those that got the softer parts to feed on were well fed. But the three that did not turned all their energies on the frame of the Gobbler, and over that there waged a battle royal. This way and that they tugged and tussled, getting off occasional scraps, but really hindering each other feeding, till Tito glided in and deftly cut the Turkey into three or four, when each dashed off with a prize, over which he sat and chewed and smacked his lips and jammed his head down sideways to bring the backmost teeth to bear, while the baby runt scrambled into the home den, carrying in triumph his share—the Gobbler's grotesque head and neck.

X

Jake felt that he had been grievously wronged, indeed ruined, by that Coyote that stole his Turkeys. He vowed he would skin them alive when he found the pups, and took pleasure in thinking about how he would do it. His attempt to follow Saddleback by trailing was a failure, and all his searching for the den was useless, but he had come prepared for any emergency. In case he found the den he had brought a pick and shovel; in case he did not he had brought a living white Hen.

The Hen he now took to a broad open place near where he had seen Saddleback, and there he tethered her to a stick of wood that she could barely drag. Then he made himself comfortable on a look-out that was near, and lay still to watch. The Hen, of course, ran to the end of the string, and then lay on the ground flopping stupidly. Presently the log gave enough to ease the strain, she turned by mere chance in another direction, and so, for a time, stood up to look around.

The day went slowly by, and Jake lazily stretched himself on the blanket in his spying-place. Toward evening Tito came by on a hunt. This was not surprising, for the den was only half a mile away. Tito had learned, among other rules, this, "Never show yourself on the sky-line." In former days the

Coyotes used to trot along the tops of the ridges for the sake of the chance to watch both sides. But men and guns had taught Tito that in this way you are sure to be seen. She therefore made a practice of running along near the top, and once in a while peeping over.

This was what she did that evening as she went out to hunt for the children's supper, and her keen eyes fell on the white Hen, stupidly stalking about and turning up its eyes in a wise way each time a harmless Turkey-buzzard came in sight against a huge white cloud.

Tito was puzzled. This was something new. It *looked* like game, but she feared to take any chances. She circled all around without showing herself, then decided that, whatever it might be, it was better let alone. As she passed on, a faint whiff of smoke caught her attention. She followed cautiously, and under a butte far from the Hen she found Jake's camp. His bed was there, his Horse was picketed, and on the remains of the fire was a pot which gave out a smell which she well knew about men's camps—the smell of coffee. Tito felt uneasy at this proof that a man was staying so near her home, but she went off quietly on her hunt, keeping out of sight, and Jake knew nothing of her visit.

About sundown he took in his decoy Hen, as Owls were abundant, and went back to his camp.

XI

Next day the Hen was again put out, and late that afternoon Saddleback came trotting by. As soon as his eye fell on the white Hen he stopped short, his head on one side, and gazed. Then he circled to get the wind, and went cautiously sneaking nearer, very cautiously, somewhat puzzled, till he got a whiff that reminded him of the place where he had found those Turkeys. The Hen took alarm, and tried to run away; but Saddleback made a rush, seized the Hen so fiercely that the string was broken, and away he dashed toward the home valley.

Jake had fallen asleep, but the squawk of the Hen happened to awaken him, and he sat up in time to see her borne away in old Saddleback's jaws.

As soon as they were out of sight Jake took up the white-feather trail. At first it was easily followed, for the Hen had shed plenty of plumes in her struggles; but once she was dead in Saddleback's jaws, very few feathers were dropped except where she was carried through the brush. But Jake was following quietly and certainly, for Saddleback had gone nearly in a straight line home to the little ones with the danger-ous tell-tale prize. Once or twice there was a puzzling delay when the Coyote had changed his course or gone over an open place; but one white feather was good for fifty yards, and when the daylight was gone, Jake was not two hundred yards from the hollow, in which at that very moment were the nine little pups, having a perfectly delightful time with the Hen, pulling it to pieces, feasting and growling, sneezing the white feathers from their noses or coughing them from their throats.

If a puff of wind had now blown from them toward Jake, it might have carried a flurry of snowy plumes or even the merry cries of the little revelers, and the den would have been discovered at once. But, as luck would have it, the evening lull was on, and all distant sounds were hidden by the crashing that Jake made in trying to trace his feather guides through the last thicket.

About this time Tito was returning home with a Magpie that she had captured by watching till it went to feed within the ribs of a dead Horse, when she ran across Jake's trail. Now, a man on foot is always a suspicious character in this country. She followed the trail for a little to see where he was going, and that she knew at once from the scent. How it tells her no one can say, yet all hunters know that it does. And Tito marked that it was going straight toward her home. Thrilled with new fear, she hid the bird she was carrying, then followed the trail of the man. Within a few minutes she could hear him in the thicket, and Tito realized the terrible danger that was threatening. She went swiftly, quietly around to the den hollow, came on the heedless little roisterers, after giving the signal-call, which prevented them taking alarm at her approach; but she must have had a shock when she saw how marked the hollow and the den were now, all drifted over with feathers white as snow. Then she gave the danger-call that sent them all to earth, and the little glade was still.

Her own nose was so thoroughly and always her guide that it was not likely she thought of the white-feathers being the telltale. But now she realized that a man, one she knew of old as a treacherous character, one whose scent had always meant mischief to her, that had been associated with all her own troubles and the cause of nearly all her desperate danger, was close to her darlings; was tracking them down, in a few minutes would surely have them in his merciless power.

Oh, the wrench to the mother's heart at the thought of what she could foresee! But the warmth of the mother-love lent life to the mother-wit. Having sent her little ones out of sight, and by a sign conveyed to Saddleback her alarm, she swiftly came back to the man, then she crossed before him, thinking, in her half-reasoning way, that the man *must* be following a foot-scent just as she herself would do, but would, of course, take the stronger line of tracks she was now laying. She did not realize that the failing daylight made any difference. Then she trotted to one side, and to make doubly sure of being followed, she uttered the fiercest challenge she could, just as many a time she had done to make the Dogs pursue her:

Grrr-wow-wow-wa-a-a-h,

and stood still; then ran a little nearer and did it again, and then again much nearer, and repeated her bark, she was so determined that the wolver should follow her.

Of course the wolver could see nothing of the Coyote, for the shades were falling. He had to give up the hunt anyway. His understanding of the details was as different as possible from that the Mother Coyote had, and yet it came to the same thing. He recognized that the Coyote's bark was the voice of the distressed mother trying to call him away. So he knew the brood must be close at hand, and all he now had to do was return in the morning and complete his search. So he made his way back to his camp.

XII

Saddleback thought they had won the victory. He felt secure, because the foot-scent that he might have supposed the man to be following would be stale by morning. Tito did not feel so safe. That two-legged beast was close to her home and her little ones; had barely been turned aside; might come back yet.

The wolver watered and repicketed his Horse, kindled the fire anew, made his coffee and ate his evening meal, then smoked awhile before lying down to sleep, thinking occasionally of the little woolly scalps he expected to gather in the morning.

He was about to roll up in his blanket when, out of the dark distance, there sounded the evening cry of the Coyote, the rolling challenge of more than one voice. Jake grinned in fiendish glee, and said: "There you are all right. Howl some more. I'll see you in the morning."

It was the ordinary, or rather *one* of the ordinary, camp-calls of the Coyote. It was sounded once, and then all was still. Jake soon forgot it in his loggish slumber.

The callers were Tito and Saddleback. The challenge was not an empty bluff. It had a distinct purpose behind it—to know for sure whether the enemy had any dogs with him; and because there was no responsive bark Tito knew that he had none.

Then Tito waited for an hour or so till the flickering fire had gone dead, and the only sound of life about the camp was the cropping of the grass by the picketed Horse. Tito crept near softly, so softly that the Horse did not see her till she was within twenty feet; then he gave a start that swung the tightened picket-rope up into the air, and snorted gently. Tito went quietly forward, and opening her wide gape, took the rope in, almost under her ears, between the great scissor-like back teeth, then chewed it for a few seconds. The fibers quickly frayed, and, aided by the strain the nervous Horse still kept up, the last of the strands gave way, and the Horse was free. He was not much alarmed; he knew the smell of Coyote; and after jumping three steps and walking six, he stopped.

The sounding thumps of his hoofs on the ground awoke the sleeper. He looked up, but, seeing the Horse standing there, he went calmly off to sleep again, supposing that all went well.

Tito had sneaked away, but she now returned like a shadow, avoided the sleeper, but came around, sniffed doubtfully at the coffee, and then puzzled over a tin can, while Saddleback examined the frying-pan full of "camp-sinkers" and then defiled both cakes and pan with dirt. The bridle hung on a low bush; the Coyotes did not know what it was, but just for luck they cut it into several pieces, then, taking the sacks that held Jake's bacon and flour, they carried them far away and buried them in the sand.

Having done all the mischief she could, Tito, followed by her mate, now set off for a wooded gully some miles away, where was a hole that had been made first by a Chipmunk, but enlarged by several other animals, including a Fox that had tried to dig out its occupants. Tito stopped and looked at many possible places before she settled on this. Then she set to work to dig. Saddleback had followed in a half-comprehending way, till he saw what she was doing. Then when she, tired with digging, came out, he went into the hole, and after snuffing about went on with the work, throwing out the earth between his hind legs; and when it was piled up behind he would come out and push it yet farther away.

And so they worked for hours, not a word said and yet with a sufficient comprehension of the object in view to work in relief of each other. And by the time the morning came they had a den big enough to do for their home, in case they must move, though it would not compare with the one in the grassy hollow.

XIII

It was nearly sunrise before the wolver awoke. With the true instinct of a plainsman he turned to look for his Horse. *It was gone.* What his ship is to the sailor, what wings are to the Bird, what money is to the merchant, the Horse is to the plainsman. Without it he is helpless, lost at sea, wing broken, crippled in business. Afoot on the plains is the sum of earthly terrors. Even Jake realized this, and ere his foggy wits had fully felt the shock he sighted the steed afar on a flat, grazing and stepping ever farther from the camp. At a second glance Jake noticed that the Horse was trailing the rope. If the rope had been left behind Jake would have known that it was hopeless to try to catch him; he would have finished his den-hunt and found the little Coyotes. But, with the trailing rope, there was a good chance of catching the Horse; so Jake set out to try.

Of all the maddening things there is nothing worse than to be almost, but not quite, able to catch your Horse. Do what he might, Jake could not get quite near enough to seize that short rope, and the Horse led him on and on, until at last they were well on the homeward trail.

Now Jake was afoot anyhow, so seeing no better plan, he set out to follow that Horse right back to the Ranch.

But when about seven miles were covered Jake succeeded in catching him. He rigged up a rough *jaquima* with the rope and rode barebacked in fifteen minutes over the three miles that lay between him and the Sheep-ranch, giving vent all the way to his pent-up feelings in cruel abuse of that Horse. Of course it did not do any good, and he knew that, but he considered it was heaps of satisfaction. Here Jake got a meal and borrowed a saddle and a mongrel Hound that could run a trail, and returned late in the afternoon to finish his den-hunt. Had he known it, he now could have found it without the aid of the cur, for it was really close at hand when he took up the feather-trail where he last had left it. Within one hundred yards he rose to the top of the little ridge; then just over it, almost face to face, he came on a Coyote, carrying in its mouth a large Rabbit. The Coyote leaped just at the same moment that Jake fired his revolver, and the Dog broke into a fierce yelling and dashed off in pursuit, while Jake blazed and blazed away, without effect, and wondered why the Coyote should still hang on to that Rabbit as she ran for her life with the Dog yelling at her heels. Jake followed as far as he could and fired at each chance, but scored no hit. So when they had vanished among the buttes he left the Dog to follow or come back as he pleased, while he returned to the den, which, of course, was plain enough now. Jake knew that the pups were there yet. Had he not seen the mother bringing a Rabbit for them?

So he set to work with pick and shovel all the rest of that day. There were plenty of signs that the den had inhabitants, and, duly encouraged, he dug on, and after several hours of the hardest work he had ever done, he came to the end of the den—*only to find it empty.* After cursing his luck at the first shock of disgust, he put on his strong leather glove and groped about in the nest. He felt something firm and drew it out. It was the head and neck of his own Turkey Gobbler, and that was all he got for his pains.

XIV

Tito had not been idle during the time that the enemy was Horse-hunting. Whatever Saddleback might have done, Tito would live in no fool's paradise. Having finished the new den, she trotted back to the little valley of feathers, and the first young one that came to meet her at the door of this home was a broad-headed one much like herself. She seized him by the neck and set off, carrying him across country toward the new den, a couple of miles away. Every little while she had to put her offspring down to rest and give it a chance to breathe. This made the moving slow, and the labor of transporting the pups occupied all that day, for Saddleback was not allowed to carry any of them, probably because he was too rough. Beginning with the biggest and brightest, they were carried away one at a time, and late in the afternoon only the runt was left. Tito had not only worked at digging all night, she had also trotted over thirty miles, half of it with a heavy baby to carry. But she did not rest. She was just coming out of the den, carrying her youngest in her mouth, when over the very edge of this hollow appeared the mongrel Hound, and a little way behind him Wolver Jake.

Away went Tito, holding the baby tight, and away went the Dog behind her.

Bang! bang! bang! said the revolver.

But not a shot touched her. Then over the ridge they dashed, where the revolver could not reach her, and sped across a flat, the tired Coyote and her baby, and the big fierce Hound behind her, bounding his hardest. Had she been fresh and unweighted she could soon have left the clumsy cur that now was barking furiously on her track and rather gaining than losing in the race. But she put forth all her strength, careered along a slope, where she gained a little, then down across a brushy flat where the cruel bushes robbed her of all she had gained. But again into the open they came, and the wolver, laboring far behind, got sight of them and fired again and again with his revolver, and only stirred the dust, but still it made her dodge and lose time, and it also spurred the Dog. The hunter saw the Coyote, his old acquaintance of the bobtail, carrying still, as he thought, the Jack-rabbit she had been bringing to her brood, and wondered at her strange persistence.

"Why doesn't she drop that weight when flying for her life?" But on she went and gamely bore her load over the hills, the man cursing his luck that he had not brought his Horse, and the mongrel bounding in deadly earnest but thirty feet behind her. Then suddenly in front of Tito yawned a little cut-bank gully. Tired and weighted, she dared not try the leap; she skirted around. But the Dog was fresh; he cleared it easily, and the mother's start was cut down by half.

But on she went, straining to hold the little one high above the scratching brush and the dangerous bayonet-spikes; but straining too much, for the helpless cub was choking in his mother's grip. She must lay him down or strangle him; with such a weight she could not much longer keep out of reach. She tried to give the howl for help, but her voice was muffled by the cub, now struggling for breath, and as she tried to ease her grip on him a sudden wrench jerked him from her mouth into the grass—into the power of the merciless Hound. Tito was far smaller than the Dog; ordinarily she would have held him in fear; but her little one, her baby, was the only thought now, and as the brute sprang forward to tear it in his wicked jaws, she leaped between and stood facing him with all her mane erect, her teeth exposed, and plainly showed her resolve to save her young one at any price. The Dog was not brave, only confident that he was bigger and had the man behind him. But the man was far away, and balked in his first rush at the trembling little Coyote, that tried to hide in the grass, the cur hesitated a moment, and Tito howled the long howl for help—the muster-call:

Yap-yap-yap-yah-yah-yah-h-h-h Yap-yap-yap-yah-yah-yah-h-h-h,

and made the buttes around re-echo so that Jake could not tell where it came from; but someone else there was that heard and did know whence it came.

The Dog's courage revived on hearing something like a far-away shout. Again he sprang at the little one, but again the mother balked him with her own body, and then they closed in deadly struggle. "Oh, if Saddleback would only come!" But no one came, and now she had no further chance to call. Weight is everything in a closing fight, and Tito soon went down, bravely fighting to the last, but clearly worsted; and the Hound's courage grew with the sight of victory, and all he thought of now was to finish her and then kill her helpless baby in its turn. He had no ears or eyes for any other thing, till out of the nearest sage there flashed a streak of gray, and in a trice the big-voiced coward was hurled back by a foe almost as heavy as himself—hurled back with a crippled shoulder. Dash, chop, and staunch old Saddleback sprang on him again. Tito struggled to her feet, and they closed on him together. His courage fled at once when he saw the odds, and all he wanted now was safe escape—escape from Saddleback, whose speed was like the wind, escape from Tito, whose baby's life was at stake. Not twenty jumps away did he get; not breath enough had he to howl for help to his master in the distant hills; not fifteen yards away from her little one that he meant to tear, they tore him all to bits.

And Tito lifted the rescued young one, and traveling as slowly as she wished, they reached the new-made den. There the family safely reunited, far away from danger of further attack by Wolver Jake or his kind.

And there they lived in peace till their mother had finished their training, and every one of them grew up wise in the ancient learning of the plains, wise in the later wisdom that the ranchers' war has forced upon them, and not only they, but their children's children, too. The Buffalo herds have gone; they have succumbed to the rifles of the hunters. The Antelope droves are nearly gone; Hound and lead were too much for them. The Blacktail bands have dwindled before axe and fence. The ancient dwellers of the Badlands have faded like snow under the new conditions, but the Coyotes are no more in fear of extinction. Their morning and evening song still sounds from the level buttes, as it did long years ago when every plain was a teeming land of game. They have learned the deadly secrets of traps and poisons, they know how to baffle the gunner and Hound, they have matched their wits with the hunter's wits. They have learned how to prosper in a land of man-made plenty, in spite of the worst that man can do, and it was Tito that taught them how.

A Fire-fighter's Dog

[ARTHUR QUILLER-COUCH]

This is the story of a very distinguished member of the London Fire Brigade—the dog Chance. It proves that the fascinations of fires (and who that has witnessed a fire cannot own this fascination?) extends even to the brute creation. In old Egypt, Herodotus tells us, the cats used on the occasion of a conflagration to rush forth from their burning homes, and then madly attempt to return again; and the Egyptians, who worshipped the animals, had to form a ring round to prevent their dashing past and sacrificing themselves to the flames. This may, however, be due to the cat's notorious love for home. In the case of the dog Chance another hypothesis has to be searched for.

The animal formed his first acquaintance with the brigade by following a fireman from a conflagration in Shoreditch to the central station at Watling Street. Here, after he had been petted for some time by the men, his master came for him and took him home. But the dog quickly escaped and returned to the central station on the very first opportunity. He was carried back, returned, was carried back again, and again returned.

At this point his master—"like a mother whose son *will* go to sea"—abandoned the struggle and allowed him to follow his own course. Henceforth for years he invariably went with the engine, sometimes upon the carriage itself, sometimes under the horses' legs; and always, when going uphill, running in advance, and announcing by his bark the welcome news that the fire-engine was at hand.

Arrived at the fire, he would amuse himself with pulling burning logs of wood out of the flames with his mouth, firmly impressed that he was rendering the greatest service, and clearly anxious to show the laymen that he understood all about the business. Although he had his legs broken half a dozen times, he remained faithful to the profession he had so obstinately chosen. At last, having taken a more serious hurt than usual, he was being nursed by the firemen beside the hearth, when a "call" came. At the well-known sound of the engine turning out, the poor old dog made a last effort to climb upon it, and fell back—dead.

He was stuffed, and preserved at the station for some time. But even in death he was destined to prove the friend of the brigade. For, one of the engineers having committed suicide, the firemen determined to raffle him for the benefit of the widow, and such was his fame that he realized 123 pounds 10 shillings, 9 pence, or over $615 in American money!

Scrap

[LUCIA CHAMBERLAIN]

t the gray end of the afternoon the regiment of twelve companies went through Monterey on its way to the summer camp, a mile out on the salt-meadows; and it was here that Scrap joined it.

He did not tag at the heels of the boys who tagged the last company, or rush out with the other dogs who barked at the band; but he appeared somehow independent of any surroundings, and marched, ears alert, stump tail erect, one foot in front of the tall first lieutenant who walked on the wing of Company A.

The lieutenant was self-conscious and so fresh to the service that his shoulder-straps hurt him. He failed to see Scrap, who was very small and very yellow, until, in quickening step, he stumbled over him and all but measured his long length. He aimed an accurate kick that sent Scrap flying, surprised but not vindictive, to the side lines, where he considered, his head cocked. With the scratched ear pricked and the bitten ear flat, he passed the regiment in review until Company K, with old Muldoon, sergeant on the flank, came by.

As lean, as mongrel, as tough, and as scarred as Scrap, he carried his wiry body with a devil-may-care assurance, in which Scrap may have recognized a kindred spirit. He decided in a flash. He made a dart and fell in abreast the sergeant of Company K. Muldoon saw and growled at him.

"Gr-r-r-r!" said Scrap, not ill-naturedly, and fell back a pace. But he did not slink. He had the secret of success. He kept as close as he could and yet escape Muldoon's boot. With his head high, ears stiff, tail up, he stepped out to the music.

Muldoon looked back with a threat that sent Scrap retreating, heels over ears. The sergeant was satisfied that the dog had gone; but when camp was reached and ranks were broken he found himself confronted by a disreputable yellow cur with a ragged ear cocked over his nose.

"Well, I'm domned!" said Muldoon. His heart, probably the toughest thing about him, was touched by this fearless persistence.

"Ar-ren't ye afraid o' nothin', ye little scrap?" he said. Scrap, answering the first name he had ever known, barked shrilly.

"What's that dog doing here?" said the tall lieu-tenant of Company A, disapprovingly.

"I'm afther kickin' him out, sor," explained Mul-doon, and, upon the lieutenant's departure, was seen retreating in the direction of the cook-tent, with the meager and expectant Scrap inconspicuously at his heels.

He went to sleep at taps in Muldoon's tent, curled up inside Muldoon's cartridge-belt; but at reveille the next morning the sergeant missed him. Between drill and drill Muldoon sought diligently, with insin-uations as to the character of dog-stealers that were near to precipitating personal conflict. He found the stray finally, in Company B street, leaping for bones amid the applause of the habitants.

Arraigned collectively as thieves, Company B declared that the dog had strayed in and remained only because he could not be kicked out. But their pride in the height of his leaps was too evidently the pride of possession; and Muldoon, after vain attempts to catch the excited Scrap, who was eager only for bones, retired with threats of some vague disaster to befall Company B the next day if *his* dog were not returned.

The responsibility, with its consequences, was taken out of Company B's hands by Scrap's depar-ture from their lines immediately after supper. He was not seen to go. He slid away silently, among the broken shadows of the tents. Company B reviled Muldoon. Scrap spent the night in a bugler's cape, among a wilderness of brasses, and reappeared the next morning at guard mount, deftly following the stately maneuvers of the band.

"Talk about a dorg's gratitude!" said the sergeant of Company B, bitterly, remembering Scrap's entertainment of the previous evening.

"I'm on to his game!" muttered old Muldoon. "Don't ye see, ye fool, he don't belong to any *wan* of us. He belongs to the crowd—to the regiment. That's what he's tryin' to show us. He's what that Frinchman down in F calls a—a mascot; and, be jabers, he moves like a soldier!"

The regiment's enthusiasm for Scrap, as voiced by Muldoon, was not extended to the commanding officer, who felt that the impressiveness of guard mount was detracted from by Scrap's deployments. Also the tall lieutenant of Company A disliked the sensation of being accompanied in his social excursions among ladies who had driven out to band practice by a lawless yellow pup with a bitten ear. The lieutenant, good fellow at bottom, was yet a bit of a snob, and he would have preferred the colonel's foolish Newfoundland to the spirited but unregenerate Scrap.

But the privates and "non-coms" judged by the spirit, and bid for the favor of their favorite, and lost money at canteen on the next company to be

distinguished as Scrap's temporary entertainers. He
was cordial, even demonstrative, but royally impartial, devoting a day to a company with a method
that was military. He had personal friends,—Muldoon for one, the cook for another,—but there was
no man in the regiment who could expect Scrap to
run to his whistle.

Yet independent as he was of individuals, he
obeyed regimental regulations like a soldier. He
learned the guns and the bugles, what actions were
signified by certain sounds. He was up in the morning with the roll of the drums. He was with every
drill that was informal enough not to require the
presence of the commanding officer, and during
dress parade languished, lamenting, in Muldoon's
tent. Barking furiously, he was the most enthusiastic
spectator of target practice. He learned to find the
straying balls when the regimental nine practiced
during "release," and betrayed a frantic desire to
"retrieve" the shot that went crashing seaward from
the sullen-mouthed cannon on the shore. More than
once he made one of the company that crossed the
lines at an unlawful hour to spend a night among the
crooked ways of Monterey.

The regiment was tiresome with tales of his tricks.
The height of his highest leap was registered in the
mess, and the number of rats that had died in his
teeth were an ever increasing score in the canteen.

He was fairly aquiver with the mere excitement and curiosity of living. There was no spot in the camp too secure or too sacred for Scrap to penetrate. His invasions were without impertinence; but the regiment was his, and he deposited dead rats in the lieutenant's shoes as casually as he concealed bones in the French horn; and slumbered in the major's hatbox with the same equanimity with which he slept in Muldoon's jacket.

The major evicted Scrap violently, but, being a good-natured man, said nothing to the colonel, who was not. But it happened, only a day after the episode of the hat-box, that the colonel entered his quarters to find the yellow mascot, fresh from a plunge in the surf and a roll in the dirt, reposing on his overcoat.

To say that the colonel was angry would be weak; but, overwhelmed as he was, he managed to find words and deeds. Scrap fled with a sharp yelp as a boot-tree caught him just above the tail.

His exit did not fail to attract attention in the company street. The men were uneasy, for the colonel was noticeably a man of action as well as of temper. Their premonitions were fulfilled when at assembly the next morning, an official announcement was read to the attentive regiment. The colonel, who was a strategist as well as a fighter, had considered the matter more calmly overnight. He was annoyed by the multiplicity of Scrap's appearances at times and places where he was officially a nuisance. He was more than annoyed by the local paper's recent reference to "our crack yellow-dog regiment." But he knew the strength of regimental sentiment concerning Scrap and the military superstition of the mascot, and he did not want to harrow the feelings of the "summer camp" by detailing a firing squad. Therefore he left a loop-hole for Scrap's escape alive. The announcement read: "All dogs found in camp not wearing collars will be shot, by order of the commanding officer."

Now there were but two dogs in camp, and the colonel's wore a collar. The regiment heard the order with consternation.

"That'll fix it," said the colonel, comfortably.

"Suppose some one gets a collar?" suggested the major, with a hint of hopefulness in his voice.

"I know my regiment," said the colonel. "There isn't enough money in it three days before pay day to buy a button. They'll send him out to-night."

Immediately after drill there was a council of war in Muldoon's tent, Muldoon holding Scrap between his knees. Scrap's scratched ear, which habitually stood cocked, flopped forlornly; his stump tail drooped dismally. The atmosphere of anxiety oppressed his sensitive spirit. He desired to play, and Muldoon only sat and rolled his argumentative tongue. From this conference those who had been present went about the business of the day with a preternatural gloom that gradually permeated the regiment. The business of the day was varied, since the next day was to be a field day, with a review in the morning and cavalry maneuvers in the afternoon.

All day Scrap was conspicuous in every quarter of the camp, but at supper-time the lieutenant of Company A noted his absence from his habitual place at the left of Muldoon in the men's mess-tent. The lieutenant was annoyed by his own anxiety.

"Of course they'll get him out, sir?" he said to the major.

"Of course," the major assented, with more confidence than he felt. The colonel was fairly irritable in his uncertainty over it.

Next morning the sentries, who had been most strictly enjoined to vigilant observation, reported that no one had left camp that night, though a man on beat four must have failed in an extraordinary way to see a private crossing his line six feet in front of him.

The muster failed to produce any rag-eared, stub-tailed, eager-eyed, collarless yellow cub. Nor did the mess-call raise his shrill bark in the vicinity of the cook's tent. The lieutenant felt disappointed.

He thought that the regiment should at least have made some sort of demonstration in Scrap's defense. It seemed a poor return for such confidence

and loyalty to be hustled out of the way on an official threat.

It seemed to him the regiment was infernally
light-hearted, as, pipe-clay white and nickel bright
in the morning sun, it swung out of camp for the
parade-ground, where the dog-carts and runabouts
and automobiles were gathering from Del Monte
and the cottages along the shore.

The sight of the twelve companies moving across
the field with the step of one warmed the cockles of
the colonel's pride. The regiment came to parade
rest, and the band went swinging past their front, past
the reviewing-stand. As it wheeled into place, the
colonel, who had been speaking to the adjutant, who
was the lieutenant of Company A, bit his sentence in
the middle, and glared at something that moved,
glittering, at the heels of the drum-major.

The colonel turned bright red. His glass fell out of
his eye-socket.

"What the devil is the matter with that dog?" he
whispered softly. And the adjutant, who had also
seen and was suffocating, managed to articulate,
"Collars!"

The colonel put his glass back in his eye. His
shoulders shook. He coughed violently as he
addressed the adjutant:

"Have that dog removed—no, let him alone—no,
adjutant, bring him here!"

So the adjutant, biting his lip, motioned Muldoon to fall out.

Tough old Muldoon tucked Scrap, struggling, squirming, glittering like a hardware shop, under his arm, and saluted his commander, while the review waited.

The colonel was blinking through his glass and trying not to grin.

"Sergeant, how many collars has that dog got on?"

"Thirteen, sor," said Muldoon.

"What for?" said the colonel, severely.

"Wan for each company, sor, an' wan for the band."

Carlo, the Soldiers' Dog

[**RUSH C. HAWKINS**]

The Ninth New York Volunteers was organized in April 1861, in the City of New York. Two of the companies were made up of men from outside the city. C was composed of men from Hoboken and Paterson, New Jersey, and G marched into the regimental headquarters fully organized from the town of Fort Lee in that State. With this last named company came Carlo, the subject of this sketch.

When he joined the regiment, he had passed beyond the period of puppyhood and was in the full flush of dogly beauty. He was large, not very large,—would probably have turned the scales at about fifty pounds. His build was decidedly "stocky," and, as horsy men would say, his feet were well under him; his chest was broad and full, back straight, color a warm dark brindle, nose and lips very black, while he had a broad, full forehead and a wonderful pair of large, round, soft, dark-brown eyes. Add to this description an air of supreme, well-bred dignity, and you have an idea of one of the noblest animals that ever lived.

His origin was obscure; one camp reunion asserted that he was born on board of a merchant ship while his mother was making a passage from Calcutta to New York; and another told of a beautiful mastiff living somewhere in the State of New Jersey that had the honor of bringing him into the world. It would be very interesting to know something of the parentage of our hero, but since the facts surrounding his birth are unattainable, we must content ourselves with telling a portion of a simple story of a good and noble life. It may be safe to assert that he was not a Native American; if he had been, he would have provided himself with the regulation genealogical tree and family coat-of-arms.

During the first part of his term of service, Carlo was very loyal to his company, marched, messed, and slept with it; but he was not above picking up, here and there, from the mess tents of the other companies a tidbit, now and then, which proved acceptable to a well-appointed digestion.

His first turn on guard was performed as a member of the detail from Co. G, and always afterward, in

the performance of that duty, he was most faithful.
No matter who else might be late, he was ever on
time when the call for guard mount was sounded,
ready to go out with his own particular squad. At
first, he would march back to company quarters
with the old detail, but, as soon as he came to realize
the value and importance of guard duty, he made up
his mind that his place was at the guard tent and on
the patrol beat, where he could be of the greatest
service in watching the movements of the enemy.

In the performance of his duties as a member of
the guard he was very conscientious and ever on the
alert. No stray pig, wandering sheep, or silly calf
could pass in front of his part of the line without
being investigated by him. It is possible that his vig-
ilance in investigating intruding meats was sharp-
ened by the hope of substantial recognition in the
way of a stray rib extracted from the marauding
offender whose ignorance of army customs in time
of war had brought it too near our lines.

As a rule, Carlo, what with his guard duties and
other purely routine items, managed to dispose of
the day until dress parade. At that time he appeared
at his best, and became the regimental dog.

No officer or soldier connected with the command
more fully appreciated "The pomp and circumstance
of great and glorious war" than he. As the band
marched out to take position previous to playing for

the companies to assemble, he would place himself alongside the drum-major, and, when the signal for marching was given, would move off with stately and solemn tread, with head well up, looking straight to the front. Upon those great occasions, he fully realized the dignity of his position, and woe betide any unhappy other dog that happened to get in front of the marching band. When upon the parade field, he became, next to the colonel, the commanding officer, and ever regarded himself as the regulator of the conduct of those careless and frivolous dogs, that go about the world like street urchins, having no character for respectability or position in society to sustain.

Of those careless ne'er-do-wells the company had accumulated a very large following. As a rule, they were harmless and companionable, and were always on hand ready for a free lunch. It was only on dress parade that they made themselves over-officious. Each company was attended to the parade ground by its particular family of canine companions, and, when all of them had assembled, the second battalion of the regiment would make itself known by a great variety of jumpings, caperings, barks of joy, and cries of delight. To this unseasonable hilarity Carlo seriously objected, and his actions plainly told the story of his disgust at the conduct of the silly members of his race. He usually remained a passive observer until the exercise in the manual of arms, at which particular period in the ceremonies, the caperings and the barkings would become quite unendurable. Our hero would then assume the character of a preserver of the peace. He would make for the nearest group of revelers, and, in as many seconds, give a half dozen or more of them vigorous shakes, which would set them to howling, and warn the others of the thoughtless tribe of an impending danger. Immediately the offenders would all scamper to another part of the field, and remain quiet until the dress parade was over. This duty was self-imposed and faithfully performed upon many occasions.

After the parade was dismissed Carlo would march back to quarters with his own company, where he would remain until the last daily distributions of rations, whereupon, after having disposed of his share, he would start out upon a tour of regimental inspection, making friendly calls at various company quarters and by taps turning up at the headquarters of the guard. His duties ended for the day, he would enjoy his well-earned rest until reveille, unless some event of an unusual nature, occurring during the night, disturbed his repose and demanded his attention.

During the first year of his service in the field, Carlo was very fortunate. He had shared in all the transportations by water, in all the marchings, skirmishes, and battles, without receiving a scratch or having a day's illness. But his good fortune was soon to end, for it was ordained that, like other brave defenders, he was to suffer in the great cause for which all were risking their lives.

The morning of April 18, 1862, my brigade, then stationed at Roanoke Island, embarked upon the steamer *Ocean Wave* for an expedition up the Elizabeth River, the object of which was to destroy the locks of the Dismal Swamp canal in order to prevent several imaginary iron-clads from getting into Albemarle Sound.

Among the first to embark was the ever ready and faithful Carlo, and the next morning, when his companions disembarked near Elizabeth City, he was one of the first to land, and, during the whole of the long and dreary march of thirty miles to Camden Court House, lasting from three o'clock in the morning until one in the afternoon, he was ever on the alert, but keeping close to his regiment. The field of battle was reached; the engagement, in which his command met with a great loss, commenced and ended, and, when the particulars of the disaster were inventoried, it was ascertained that a Confederate bullet had taken the rudimentary claw from Carlo's left fore-leg. This was his first wound, and he bore it like a hero without a whine or even a limp. A private of Co. G, who first noticed the wound, exclaimed: "Ah, Carlo, what a pity you are not an officer! If you were, the loss of that claw would give you sixty days' leave and a brigadier general's commission at the end of it." That was about the time that generals' commissions had become very plentiful in the Department of North Carolina.

The command re-embarked, and reached Roanoke Island the morning after the engagement, in time for the regulation "Hospital or Sick Call," which that day brought together an unusual number of patients, and among them Carlo, who was asked to join the waiting line by one of the wounded men. When his turn came to be inspected by the attending surgeon, he was told to hold up the wounded leg, which he readily did, and then followed the washing, the application of simple cerate, and the bandaging, with a considerable show of interest and probable satisfaction.

Thereafter, there was no occasion to ask him to attend the surgeon's inspection. Each morning, as soon as the bugle call was sounded, he would take his place in line with the other patients, advance in his turn, and receive the usual treatment. This habit continued until the wound was healed.

Always, after this, to every friendly greeting, he would respond by holding up the wounded leg for inspection, and he acted as though he thought that everybody was interested in the honorable scar that told the story of patriotic duty faithfully performed.

Later on, for some reason known to himself, Carlo transferred his special allegiance to Co. K. and maintained close connection with that company until the end of his term of service. He was regarded by its members as a member of the company mess, and was treated as one of them. But, notwithstanding his special attachments, there can be no reasonable doubt about his having considered himself a member of the regiment, clothed with certain powers and responsibilities. At the end of his term he was fitted with a uniform—trousers, jacket, and fez, and, thus dressed, he marched up Broadway, immediately behind the band. He was soon after mustered out of the service, and received an honorable discharge, not signed with written characters, but attested by the good-will of every member of the regiment.

Bruce

[ALBERT PAYSON TERHUNE]

"Yes, ir's an easy enough trade to pick up," lectured Top Sergeant Mahan, formerly of the regular army. "You've just got to remember a few things. But you've got to keep on remembering those few, all the time. If you forget one of 'em, it's the last bit of forgetting you're ever likely to do."

Top Sergeant Mahan, of the mixed French-and-American regiment known as "Here We Come," was squatting at ease on the trench firing-step. From that professorial seat he was dispensing useful knowledge to a group of fellow-countrymen—newly arrived from the base, to pad the "Here-We-Come" ranks, which had been thinned at the Rache attack.

"What sort of things have we got to remember, Sergeant?" jauntily asked a lanky Missourian. "We've got the drill pretty pat; and the trench instructions and——"

"Gee!" ejaculated Mahan. "I had no idea of that! Then why don't you walk straight ahead into Berlin? If you know all you say you do, about war, there's nothing more for you to learn. I'll drop a line to General Foch and suggest to him that you rookies be detailed to teach the game to us oldsters."

"I didn't mean to be fresh," apologized the jaunty one. "Won't you go ahead and tell us the things we need to remember?"

"Well," exhorted Mahan, appeased by the new-comer's humility, "there aren't so many of them, after all. Learn to duck, when you hear a Minnie grunt or a whizz-bang cut loose; or a five-nine begin to whimper. Learn not to bother to duck when the rifles get to jabbering—for you'll never hear the bullet that gets you. Study the nocturnal habits of machine-guns and the ways of snipers and the right time not to play the fool. And keep saying to yourself: 'The bullet ain't molded that can get *me*!' Mean it when you say it. When you've learned those few things, the rest of the war-game is dead easy."

"Except," timidly amended old Sergeant Vivier, the gray little Frenchman, "except when eyes are—are what you call it, no use."

"That's right," assented Mahan. "In the times when eyes are no use, all rules fail. And then the only thing you can do is to trust to your Yankee luck. I remember—"

"'When eyes are no use'?" repeated the recruit. "If you mean after dark, at night—haven't we got the searchlights and the starshells and all that?"

"Son," replied Mahan, "we have. Though I don't see how you ever guessed such an important secret. But since you know everything, maybe you'll just kindly tell us what good all the lights in the world are going to do us when the filthy yellow-gray fog begins to ooze up out of the mud and the shell-holes, and the filthy gray mist oozes down from the clouds to meet it. Fog is the one thing that all the war-science won't overcome. A fog-penetrator hasn't been invented yet. If it had been, there'd be many a husky lad living today, who has gone West, this past few years, on account of the fogs. Fog is the boche's pet. It gives Fritzy a lovely chance to creep up on us. It—"

"It is the helper of *us,* too," suggested old Vivier. "More than one time, it has kept me safe when I was on patrol. And did it not help to save us at Rache, when—"

"The fog may have helped us, one per cent, at Rache," admitted Mahan. "But Bruce did ninety-nine per cent of the saving."

"A Scotch general?" asked the recruit, as Vivier nodded cordial affirmation of Mahan's words, and as others of the old-timers muttered approval.

"No," contradicted Mahan. "A Scotch collie. If you were dry behind the ears, in this life, you wouldn't have to ask who Bruce is."

"I don't understand," faltered the rookie, suspicious of a possible joke.

"You will soon," Mahan told him. "Bruce will be here to-day. I heard the K.O. saying the big dog is going to be sent down with some dispatches or something, from headquarters. It's his first trip since he was cut up so."

"I am saving him—this!" proclaimed Vivier, disgorging from the flotsam of his pocket a lump of once-white sugar. "My wife, she smuggle three of these to me in her last *paquet*. One I eat in my *café noir;* one I present to *mon cher vieux, ce bon* Mahan; one I keep for the grand dog what save us all that day."

"What's the idea?" queried the mystified rookie. "I don't—"

"We were stuck in the front line of the Rache salient," explained Mahan, eager to recount his dog-friend's prowess. "On both sides our supports got word to fall back. We couldn't get the word, because our telephone connection was knocked galley-west. There we were, waiting for a Hun attack to wipe us out. We couldn't fall back, for they were peppering the hill-slope behind us. We were at the bottom. They'd have cut us to ribbons if we'd shown our carcasses in the open. Bruce was here, with a message he'd brought. The K.O. sent him back to headquarters for the reserves. The boche heavies and snipers and machine-guns all cut loose to stop him as he scooted up the hill. And a measly giant of a German police dog tried to kill him, too. Bruce got through the lot of them; and he reached headquarters with the S.O.S. call that saved us. The poor chap was cut and gouged and torn by bullets and shell-scraps, and he was nearly dead from shell-shock, too. But the surgeon-general worked over him, himself, and pulled him back to life. He—"

"He is a loved pet of a man and a woman in your America, I have heard one say," chimed in Vivier. "And his home, there, was in the quiet country. He was lent to the cause, as a patriotic offering, *ce brave*! And of a certainty, he has earned his welcome."

When Bruce, an hour later, trotted into the trenches, on the way to the "Here-We-Come" colonel's quarters, he was received like a visiting potentate. Dozens of men hailed him eagerly by name as he made his way to his destination with the message affixed to his collar.

Many of these men were his well-remembered friends and comrades. Mahan and Vivier, and one or two more, he had grown to like—as well as he could like any one in that land of horrors, three thousand miles away from The Place, where he was born, and from the Mistress and the Master, who were his loyally worshiped gods.

Moreover, being only mortal and afflicted with a hearty appetite, Bruce loved the food and other delicacies the men were forever offering him as a variation on the stodgy fare dished out to him and his fellow-war-dogs.

As much to amuse and interest the soldiers whose hero he was, as for any special importance in the dispatch he carried, Bruce had been sent now to the trenches of the "Here-We-Comes." It was his first visit to the regiment he had saved, since the days of the Rache assault two months earlier. Thanks to supremely clever surgery and to tender care, the dog was little the worse for his wounds. His hearing gradually had come back. In one shoulder he had a very slight stiffness which was not a limp, and a new-healed furrow scarred the left side of his tawny coat. Otherwise he was as good as new.

As Bruce trotted toward the group that so recently had been talking of him, the Missouri recruit watched with interest for the dog's joy at this reunion with his old friends. Bruce's snowy chest and black-stippled coat were fluffed out by many recent baths. His splendid head high and his dark eyes bright, the collie advanced toward the group.

Mahan greeted him joyously. Vivier stretched out a hand which displayed temptingly the long-hoarded lump of sugar. A third man produced, from nowhere in particular, a large and meat-fringed soup-bone.

"I wonder which of you he'll come to, first," said the interested Missourian.

The question was answered at once, and right humiliatingly. For Bruce did not falter in his swinging stride as he came abreast of the group. Not by so much as a second glance did he notice Mahan's hail and the tempting food.

As he passed within six inches of the lump of sugar which Vivier was holding out to him, the dog's silken ears quivered slightly,—sure sign of hard-repressed emotion in a thoroughbred collie,—but he gave no other manifestation that he knew any one was there.

"Well, I'll be blessed!" snickered the Missourian in high derision, as Bruce passed out of sight around an angle of the trench. "So *that's* the pup who is such a pal of you fellows, is he? Gee, but it was a treat to see how tickled he was to meet you again!"

To the rookie's amazement none of his hearers seemed in the least chagrined over the dog's chilling disregard of them. Instead, Mahan actually grunted approbation.

"He'll be back," prophesied the Sergeant. "Don't you worry. He'll be back. We ought to have had more sense than try to stop him when he's on duty. He has better discipline than the rest of us. That's one of very first things they teach a courier-dog—to pay no attention to anybody, when he's on dispatch duty. When Bruce has delivered his message to the K.O., he'll have the right to hunt up his chums. And no one knows it better'n Bruce himself."

"It was a sin—a thoughtlessness—of me to hold the sugar at him," said old Vivier. "Ah, but he is a so good soldier, *ce brave* Bruce! He look not to the left nor yet to the right, nor yet to the so-desired sugar-lump. He keep his head at attention! All but the furry tips of his ears. Them he has not yet taught to be good soildiers. They tremble, when he smell the sugar and the good soup-bone. They quiver like the little leaf. But he keep on. He—"

There was a scurry of fast-cantering feet. Around the angle of the trench dashed Bruce. Head erect, soft dark eyes shining with a light of gay mischief, he galloped up to the grinning Sergeant Vivier and stood. The dog's great plume of a tail was wagging violently. His tulip ears were cocked. His whole interest in life was fixed on the precious lump of sugar which Vivier held out to him.

From puppyhood, Bruce had adored lump sugar. Even at The Place, sugar had been a rarity for him, for the Mistress and the Master had known the damage it can wreak upon a dog's teeth and digestion. Yet, once in a while, as a special luxury, the Mistress had been wont to give him a solitary lump of sugar.

Since his arrival in France, the dog had never seen nor scented such a thing until now. Yet he did not jump for the gift. He did not try to snatch it from Vivier. Instead, he waited until the old Frenchman held it closer toward him, with the invitation:

"Take it, *mon vieux*! It is for you."

Then and then only did Bruce reach daintily forward and grip the grimy bit of sugar between his mighty jaws. Vivier stroked the collie's head while Bruce wagged his tail and munched the sugar and blinked gratefully up at the donor. Mahan looked on, enviously.

"A dog's got forty-two teeth, instead of the thirty-two that us humans have to chew on," observed the Sergeant. "A vet' told me that once. And sugar is bad for all forty-two of 'em. Maybe you didn't know that, Monsoo Vivier? Likely, at this rate, we'll have to chip in before long and buy poor Brucie a double set of false teeth. Just because you've put his real ones out of business with lumps of sugar!"

Vivier looked genuinely concerned at this grim forecast. Bruce wandered across to the place where the donor of the soup-bone brandished his offering. Other men, too, were crowding around with gifts.

Between petting and feeding, the collie spent a busy hour among his comrades-at-arms. He was to stay with the "Here-We-Comes" until the following day, and then carry back to headquarters a reconnaissance report.

At four o'clock that afternoon the sky was softly blue and the air was unwontedly clear. By five o'clock a gentle India-summer haze blurred the world's sharper outlines. By six a blanket-fog rolled in, and the air was wetly unbreatheable. The fog lay so thick over the soggy earth that objects ten feet away were invisible.

"This," commented Sergeant Mahan, "is one of the times I was talking about this morning—when eyes are no use. This is sure the country for fogs, in war-time. The cockneys tell me the London fogs aren't a patch on 'em."

The "Here-We-Comes" were encamped, for the while, at the edge of a sector from whence all military importance had recently been removed by a convulsive twist of a hundred-mile battle-front. In this dull hole-in-a-corner the new-arrived rivets were in process of welding into the more veteran structure of the mixed regiment.

Not a quarter-mile away—across No Man's Land and athwart two barriers of barbed wire—lay a series of German trenches. Now, in all probability, and from all outward signs, the occupants of this boche position consisted only of a regiment or two which had been so badly cut up, in a foiled drive, as to need a month of non-exciting routine before going back into more perilous service.

Yet the commander of the division to which the "Here-We-Comes" were attached did not trust to probabilities nor to outward signs. He had been at the front long enough to realize that the only thing likely to happen was the thing which seemed unlikeliest. And he felt a morbid curiosity to learn more about the personnel of those dormant German trenches.

Wherefore he had sent an order that a handful of the "Here-We-Comes" go forth into No Man's Land, on the first favorable night, and try to pick up a boche prisoner or two for questioning-purposes. A scouring of the doubly wired area between the hostile lines might readily harvest some solitary sentinel or some other man on special duty, or even the occupants of a listening-post. And the division commander earnestly desired to question such prisoner or prisoners. The fog furnished an ideal night for such an expedition.

Thus it was that a very young lieutenant and Sergeant Mahan and ten privates—the lanky Missourian among them—were detailed for the prisoner-seeking job. At eleven o'clock, they crept over the top, single file.

It was a night wherein a hundred searchlights and a million star-flares would not have made more impression on the density of the fog than would the striking of a safety match. Yet the twelve reconnoiterers were instructed to proceed in the cautious manner customary to such nocturnal expeditions into No Man's Land. They moved forward at the lieutenant's order, tiptoeing abreast, some twenty feet apart from one another, and advancing in three-foot strides. At every thirty steps the entire line was required to halt and to reestablish contact—in other words, to "dress" on the lieutenant, who was at the extreme right.

This maneuver was more time-wasting and less simple than its recital would imply. For in the dark, unaccustomed legs are liable to miscalculation in the matter of length of stride, even when shell-holes and other inequalities of ground do not complicate the calculations still further. And it is hard to maintain a perfectly straight line when moving forward through choking fog and over scores of obstacles.

The halts for realignment consumed much time and caused no little confusion. Nervousness began to encompass the Missouri recruit. He was as brave as the next man. But there is something creepy about walking with measured tread through an invisible space, with no sound but the stealthy *pad-pad-pad* of equally hesitant footsteps twenty feet away on either side. The Missourian was grateful for the intervals that brought the men into mutual contact, as the eerie march continued.

The first line of barbed wire was cut and passed. Then followed an endless groping progress across No Man's Land, and several delays, as one man or another had trouble in finding contact with his neighbor.

At last the party came to the German wires. The lieutenant had drawn on a rubber glove. In his gloved hand he grasped a strip of steel which he held in front of him, like a wand, fanning the air with it.

As he came to the entanglement, he probed the barbed wire carefully with his wand, watching for an ensuing spark. For the Germans more than once had been known to electrify their wires, with fatal results to luckless prowlers.

These wires, to-night, were not charged. And, with pliers, the lieutenant and Mahan started to cut a passageway through them.

As the very first strand parted under his pressure, Mahan laid one hand warningly on the lieutenant's sleeve, and then passed the same prearranged warning down the line to the left.

Silence—moveless, tense, sharply listening silence— followed his motion. Then the rest of the party heard the sound which Mahan's keener ears had caught a moment earlier—the thud of many marching feet.

Here was no furtive creeping, as when the twelve Yankees had moved along. Rather was it the rhythmic beat of at least a hundred pairs of shapeless army boots—perhaps of more. The unseen marchers were moving wordlessly, but with no effort at muffling the even tread of their multiple feet.

"They're coming this way!" breathed Sergeant Mahan almost without sound, his lips close to the excited young lieutenant's ear. "And they're not fifty paces off. That means they're boches. So near the German wire, *our* men would either be crawling or else charging, not marching! It's a company— maybe a battalion—coming back from a reconnaissance, and making for a gap in their own wire somewhere near here. If we lay low there's an off chance they may pass us by."

Without awaiting the lieutenant's order, Mahan passed along the signal for every man to drop to earth and lie there. He all but forced the eagerly gesticulating lieutenant to the ground.

On came the swinging tread of the Germans. Mahan, listening breathlessly, tried to gauge the distance and the direction. He figured, presently, that the break the Germans had made in their wire could be only a few yards below the spot where he and the lieutenant had been at work with the pliers. Thus the intruders, from their present course, must inevitably pass very close to the prostrate Americans—so close, perhaps, as to brush against the nearest of them, or even to step on one or more of the crouching figures.

Mahan whispered to the man on his immediate left, the rookie from Missouri:

"Edge closer to the wire—close as you can wiggle, and lie flat. Pass on the word."

The Missourian obeyed. Before writhing his long body forward against the bristly mass of wire he passed the instructions on to the man at his own left.

But his nerves were at breaking-point.

It had been bad enough to crawl through the blind fog, with the ghostly steps of his comrades pattering softly at either side of him. But it was a thousand times harder to lie helpless here, in the choking fog and on the soaked ground, while countless enemies were bearing down, unseen, upon him, on one side, and an impenetrable wire cut off his retreat on the other.

The Missourian had let his imagination begin to work—always a mistake in a private soldier. He was visualizing the moment when this tramping German force should become aware of the presence of their puny foes and should slaughter them against the merciless wires. It would not be a fair stand-up fight, this murder-rush of hundreds of men against twelve who were penned in and could not maneuver nor escape. And the thought of it was doing queer things to the rookie's overwrought nerves.

Having passed the word to creep closer to the wires, he began to execute the order in person, with no delay at all. But he was a fraction of a second too late. The Germans were moving in hike-formation with "points" thrown out in advance to either side—a "point" being a private soldier who, for scouting and other purposes, marches at some distance from the main body.

The point, ahead of the platoon, had swerved too far to the left, in the blackness—an error that would infalliby have brought him up against the wires, with considerable force, in another two steps. But the Missourian was between him and the wires. And the point's heavy-shod foot came down, heel first, on the back of the rookie's out-groping hand. Such a crushing impact, on the hand-back, is one of the most agonizing minor injuries a man can sustain. And this fact the Missourian discovered with great suddenness.

His too-taut nerves forced from his throat a yell that split the deathly stillness with an ear-piercing vehemence. He sprang to his feet, forgetful of orders—intent only on thrusting his bayonet through the Hun who had caused such acute torture to his hand. Halfway up, the rookie's feet went out from under him in the slimy mud. He caromed against the point, then fell headlong.

The German, doubtless thinking he had stumbled upon a single stray American scout, whirled his own rifle aloft, to dash out the brains of his luckless foe. But before the upflung butt could descend,—before the rookie could rise or dodge,—the point added his quota to the rude breaking of the night's silence. He screamed in panic terror, dropped his brandished gun and reeled backward, clawing at his own throat.

For out of the eerie darkness, something had launched itself at him—something silent and terrible, that had flown to the Missourian's aid. Down with a crash went the German, on his back. He rolled against the Missourian, who promptly sought to grapple with him.

But even as he clawed for the German, the rookie's nerves wrung from him a second yell—this time less of rage than of horror.

"Sufferin' cats!" he bellowed. "Why didn't anybody ever tell me Germans was covered with fur instead of clothes?"

The boche platoon was no longer striding along in hike-formation. It was broken up into masses of wildly running men, all of them bearing down upon the place whence issued this ungodly racket and turmoil. Stumbling, reeling, blindly falling and rising again, they came on.

Some one among them loosed a rifle-shot in the general direction of the yelling. A second and a third German rifleman followed the example of the first. From the distant American trenches, one or two snipers began to pepper away toward the enemy lines, though the fog was too thick for them to see the German rifle-flashes.

The boches farthest to the left, in the blind rush, fouled with the wires. German snipers, from behind the Hun parapets, opened fire. A minute earlier the night had been still as the grave. Now it fairly vibrated with clangor. All because one rookie's nerves had been less stanch than his courage, and because that same rookie had not only had his hand stepped on in the dark, but had encountered something swirling and hairy when he grabbed for the soldier who had stepped on him!

The American lieutenant, at the onset of the clamor, sprang to his feet, whipping out his pistol; his dry lips parted in a command to charge—a command which, naturally, would have reduced his eleven men and himself to twelve corpses or to an equal number of mishandled prisoners within the next few seconds. But a big hand was clapped unceremoniously across the young officer's mouth, silencing the half-spoken suicidal order.

Sergeant Mahan's career in the regular army had given him an almost uncanny power of sizing up his fellowmen. And he had long ago decided that this was the sort of thing his untried lieutenant would be likely to do, in just such an emergency. Wherefore his flagrant breach of discipline in shoving his palm across the mouth of his superior officer.

And as he was committing this breach of discipline, he heard the Missourian's strangled gasp of:

"Why didn't anybody ever tell me Germans was covered with fur?"

In a flash Mahan understood. Wheeling, he stooped low and flung out both arms in a wide-sweeping circle. Luckily his right hand's finger-tips, as they completed the circle, touched something fast-moving and furry.

"Bruce!" he whispered fiercely, tightening his precarious grip on the wisp of fur his fingers had touched. "Bruce! Stand still, boy! It's *you* who's got to get us clear of this! Nobody else, short of the good Lord, can do it!"

Bruce had had a pleasantly lazy day with his friends in the first-line trenches. There had been much good food and more petting. And at last, comfortably tired of it all, he had gone to sleep. He had awakened in a most friendly mood, and a little hungry. Wherefore he had sallied forth in search of human companionship. He found plenty of soldiers who were more than willing to talk to him and make much of him. But, a little farther ahead, he saw his good friend, Sergeant Mahan, and other of his acquaintances, starting over the parapet on what promised to be a jolly evening stroll.

All dogs find it hard to resist the mysterious lure of a walk in human companionship. True, the night was not an ideal one for a ramble, and the fog had a way of congealing wetly on Bruce's shaggy coat. Still, a damp coat was not enough of a discomfort to offset the joy of a stroll with his friends. So Bruce had followed the twelve men quietly into No Man's Land, falling decorously into step behind Mahan.

It had not been much of a walk, for speed or for fun. For the humans went ridiculously slowly, and had an eccentric way of bunching together, every now and again, and then of stringing out into a shambling line. Still, it was a walk, and therefore better than loafing behind in the trenches. And Bruce had kept his noiseless place at the Sergeant's heels.

Then—long before Mahan heard the approaching tramp of feet—Bruce caught not only the sound but the scent of the German platoon. The scent at once told him that the strangers were not of his own army. A German soldier and an American soldier—because of their difference in diet as well as for certain other and more cogent reasons—have by no means the same odor, to a collie's trained scent, nor to that of other breeds of war-dogs. Official records of dog-sentinels prove that.

Aliens were nearing Bruce's friends. And the dog's ruff began to stand up. But Mahan and the rest seemed in no way concerned in spirit thereby— though, to the dog's understanding, they must surely be aware of the approach. So Bruce gave no further sign of displeasure. He was out for a walk, as a guest. He was not on sentry-duty.

But when the nearest German was almost upon them, and all twelve Americans dropped to the ground, the collie became interested once more. A German stepped on the hand of one of his newest friends. And the friend yelled in pain. Whereat the German made as if to strike the stepped-on man.

This was quite enough for loyal Bruce. Without so much as a growl of warning, he jumped at the offender.

Dog and man tumbled earthward together. Then after an instant of flurry and noise, Bruce felt Mahan's fingers on his shoulder and heard the stark appeal of Mahan's whispered voice. Instantly the dog was a professional soldier once more—alertly obedient and resourceful.

"Catch hold my left arm, Lieutenant!" Mahan was exhorting. "Close up, there, boys—every man's hand grabbing tight to the shoulder of the man on his left! Pass the word. And you, Missouri, hang onto the Lieutenant! Quick, there! And tread soft and tread fast, and don't let go, whatever happens! Not a sound out of any one! I'm leading the way. And Bruce is going to lead *me*."

There was a scurrying scramble as the men groped for one another. Mahan tightened his hold on Bruce's mane.

"Bruce!" he said, very low, but with a strength of appeal that was not lost on the listening dog. "Bruce! Camp! Back to *camp*! And keep *quiet*! Back to camp, boy! *Camp*!"

He had no need to repeat his command so often and so strenuously. Bruce was a trained courier. The one word "Camp!" was quite enough to tell him what he was to do.

Turning, he faced the American lines and tried to break into a gallop. His scent and his knowledge of direction were all the guides he needed. A dog always relies on his nose first and his eyes last. The fog was no obstacle at all to the collie. He understood the Sergeant's order, and he set out at once to obey it.

But at the very first step, he was checked. Mahan did not release that feverishly tight hold on his mane, but merely shifted to his collar.

Bruce glanced back, impatient at the delay. But Mahan did not let go. Instead he said once more:

"*Camp,* boy!"

And Bruce understood he was expected to make his way to camp, with Mahan hanging on to his collar.

Bruce did not enjoy this mode of locomotion. It was inconvenient, and there seemed no sense in it; but there were many things about this strenuous war-trade that Bruce neither enjoyed nor comprehended, yet which he performed at command.

So again he turned campward, Mahan at his collar and an annoyingly hindering tail of men stumbling silently on behind them. All around were the Germans—butting drunkenly through the blanket-dense fog, swinging their rifles like flails, shouting confused orders, occasionally firing. Now and then two or more of them would collide and would wrestle in blind fury, thinking they had encountered an American.

Impeded by their own sightlessly swarming numbers, as much as by the impenetrable darkness, they sought the foe. And but for Bruce they must quickly have found what they sought. Even in compact form, the Americans could not have had the sheer luck to dodge every scattered contingent of Huns which starred the German end of No Man's Land—most of them between the fugitives and the American lines.

But Bruce was on dispatch duty. It was his work to obey commands and to get back to camp at once. It was bad enough to be handicapped by Mahan's grasp on his collar. He was not minded to suffer further delay by running into any of the clumps of

gesticulating and cabbage-reeking Germans between
him and his goal. So he steered clear of such groups,
making several wide detours in order to do so. Once
or twice he stopped short to let some of the Germans grope past him, not six feet away. Again he
veered sharply to the left—increasing his pace and
forcing Mahan and the rest to increase theirs—to
avoid a squad of thirty men who were quartering
the field in close formation, and who all but jostled
the dog as they strode sightlessly by.

An occasional rifle-shot spat forth its challenge.
From both trench-lines men were firing at a venture. A few of the bullets sang nastily close to the
twelve huddled men and their canine leader. Once
a German, not three yards away, screamed aloud
and fell sprawling and kicking, as one such chance
bullet found him. Above and behind, sounded the
plop of star-shells sent up by the enemy in futile
hope of penetrating the viscid fog. And everywhere was heard the shuffle and stumbling of
innumerable boots.

At last the noise of feet began to die away, and the
uneven groping tread of the twelve Americans to
sound more distinctly for the lessening of the surrounding trumoil. And in another few seconds
Bruce came to a halt—not to an abrupt stop, as
when he had allowed an enemy squad to pass in
front of him, but a leisurely checking of speed, to

denote that he could go no farther with the load he was helping to haul.

Mahan put out his free hand. It encountered the American wires. Bruce had stopped at the spot where the party had cut a narrow path through the entanglement on the outward journey. Alone, the dog could easily have passed through the gap, but he could not be certain of pulling Mahan with him. Wherefore the halt.

The last of the twelve men scrambled down to safety, in the American first-line trench, Bruce among them. The lieutenant went straight to his commanding officer, to make his report. Sergeant Mahan went straight to his company cook, whom he woke from a snoreful sleep. Presently Mahan ran back to where the soldiers were gathered admiringly around Bruce.

The Sergeant carried a chunk of fried beef, for which he had just given the cook his entire remaining stock of cigarettes.

"Here you are, Bruce!" he exclaimed. "The best in the shop is none too good for the dog that got us safe out of that filthy mess. Eat hearty!"

Bruce did not so much as sniff at the (more or less) tempting bit of meat. Coldly he looked up at Mahan. Then, with sensitive ears laid flat against his silken head, in token of strong contempt, he turned his back on the Sergeant and walked away.

Which was Bruce's method of showing what he thought of a human fool who would give him a command and who would then hold so tightly to him that the dog could hardly carry out the order.

Three Men in a Boat

[JEROME K. JEROME]

George said:

"Let's go up the river."

He said we should have fresh air, exercise, and quiet; the constant change of scene would occupy our minds (including what there was of Harris's); and the hard work would give us a good appetite, and make us sleep well.

Harris said he didn't think George ought to do anything that would have a tendency to make him sleepier than he always was, as it might be dangerous.

He said he didn't very well understand how George was going to sleep any more than he did now, seeing that there were only twenty-four hours in each day, summer and winter alike; but thought that if he *did* sleep any more, he might just as well be dead, and so save his board and lodging.

Harris said, however, that the river would suit him to a "T." I don't know what a "T" is (except a sixpenny one, which includes bread-and-butter and cake *ad lib.,* and is cheap at the price, if you haven't had any dinner). It seems to suit everybody, however, which is greatly to its credit.

It suited me to a "T" too, and Harris and I both said it was a good idea of George's; and we said it in a tone that seemed to somehow imply that we were surprised that George should have come out so sensible.

The only one who was not struck with the suggestion was Montmorency. He never did care for the river, did Montmorency.

"It's all very well for you fellows," he says; "you like it, but I don't. There's nothing for me to do. Scenery is not in my line, and I don't smoke. If I see a rat, you won't stop; and if I go to sleep, you get fooling about with the boat, and slop me overboard. If you ask me, I call the whole thing bally foolishness." We were three to one, however, and the motion was carried. . . .

We therefore decided that we would sleep out on fine nights; and hotel it, and inn it, and pub it, like respectable folks, when it was wet, or when we felt inclined for a change.

Montmorency hailed this compromise with much approval. He does not revel in romantic solitude.

Give him something noisy; and if a trifle low, so much the jollier. To look at Montmorency you would imagine that he was an angel sent upon the earth, for some reason withheld from mankind, in the shape of a small fox-terrier. There is a sort of Oh-what-a-wicked-world-this-is-and-how-I-wish-I-could-do-something-to-make-it-better-and-nobler expression about Montmorency that has been known to bring the tears into the eyes of pious old ladies and gentlemen.

When first he came to live at my expense, I never thought I should be able to get him to stop long. I used to sit down and look at him, as he sat on the rug and looked up at me, and think: "Oh, that dog will never live. He will be snatched up to the bright skies in a chariot, that is what will happen to him."

But, when I had paid for about a dozen chickens that he had killed; and had dragged him, growling and kicking, by the scruff of his neck, out of a hundred and fourteen street fights; and had had a dead cat brought round for my inspection by an irate female, who called me a murderer; and had been summoned by the man next door but one for having a ferocious dog at large, that had kept him pinned up in his own tool-shed, afraid to venture his nose outside the door for over two hours on a cold night; and had learned that the gardener, unknown to myself, had won thirty shillings by backing him to kill rats against time, then I began to think that maybe they'd let him remain on earth for a bit longer, after all.

To hang about a stable, and collect a gang of the most disreputable dogs to be found in the town, and lead them out to march gave to the suggestion of inns, and pubs, and hotels his most emphatic approbation . . . .

Montmorency was in it all, of course. Montmorency's ambition in life, is to get in the way and be sworn at. If he can squirm in anywhere where he particularly is not wanted, and be a perfect nuisance, and make people mad, and have things thrown at his head, then he feels his day has not been wasted.

To get somebody to stumble over him, and curse him steadily for an hour, is his highest aim and object; and, when he has succeeded in accomplishing this, his conceit becomes quite unbearable.

He came and sat down on things, just when they were wanted to be packed; and he labored under the fixed belief that, whenever Harris or George reached out their hand for anything, it was his cold damp nose that they wanted. He put his leg into the jam, and he worried the teaspoons, and he pretended that the lemons were rats, and got into the hamper and killed three of them before Harris could land him with the frying-pan.

Harris said I encouraged him. I didn't encourage him. A dog like that don't want any encouragement.

It's the natural, original sin that is born in him that makes him do things like that. . . .

From Medmenham to sweet Hambledon lock the river is full of peaceful beauty, but, after it passes Greenlands, the rather uninteresting looking river residence of my newsagent—a quiet unassuming old gentleman, who may often be met with about these regions, during the summer months, sculling himself along in easy vigorous style, or chatting genially to some old lock-keeper, as he passes through—until well the other side of Henley, it is somewhat bare and dull.

We got up tolerably early on the Monday morning at Marlow, and went for a bath before breakfast; and, coming back, Montmorency made an awful ass of himself. The only subject on which Montmorency and I have any serious difference of opinion is cats. I like cats; Montmorency does not.

When I meet a cat, I say, "Poor Pussy!" and stoop down and tickle the side of its head; and the cat sticks up its tail in a rigid, cast-iron manner, arches its back, and wipes its nose up against my trousers; and all is gentleness and peace. When Montmorency meets a cat, the whole street knows about it; and there is enough bad language wasted in ten seconds to last an ordinary respectable man all his life, with care.

I do not blame the dog (contenting myself, as a rule, with merely clouting his head or throwing stones at him), because I take it that it is his nature. Fox-terriers are born with about four times as much original sin in them as other dogs are, and it will take years and years of patient effort on the part of us Christians to bring about any appreciable reformation in the rowdiness of the fox-terrier nature.

I remember being in the lobby of the Haymarket Stores one day, and all round about me were dogs, waiting for the return of their owners, who were shopping inside. There were a mastiff, and one or two collies, and a St. Bernard, a few retrievers and Newfoundlands, a boar-hound, a French poodle, with plenty of hair round its head, but mangy about the middle; a bulldog, a few Lowther Arcade sort of animals, about the size of rats, and a couple of Yorkshire tykes.

There they sat, patient, good, and thoughtful. A solemn peacefulness seemed to reign in that lobby. An air of calmness and resignation—of gentle sadness pervaded the room.

Then a sweet young lady entered, leading a meek-looking little fox-terrier, and left him, chained up there, between the bulldog and the poodle. He sat and looked about him for a minute. Then he cast up his eyes to the ceiling, and seemed, judging from his expression, to be thinking of his mother. Then he yawned. Then he looked round at the other dogs, all silent, grave, and dignified.

He looked at the bulldog, sleeping dreamlessly on his right. He looked at the poodle, erect and haughty, on his left. Then, without a word of warning, without the shadow of a provocation, he bit that poodle's near foreleg, and a yelp of agony rang through the quiet shades of that lobby.

The result of his first experiment seemed highly satisfactory to him, and he determined to go on and make things lively all round. He sprang over the poodle and vigorously attacked a collie, and the collie woke up, and immediately commenced a fierce and noisy contest with the poodle. Then Foxey came back to his own place, and caught the bulldog by the ear, and tried to throw him away; and the bulldog, a curiously impartial animal, went for everything he could reach, including the hall-porter, which gave that dear little terrier the opportunity to enjoy an uninterrupted fight of his own with an equally willing Yorkshire tyke.

Anyone who knows canine nature need hardly be told that, by this time, all the other dogs in the place were fighting as if their hearths and homes depended on the fray. The big dogs fought each other indiscriminately; and the little dogs fought among themselves, and filled up their spare time by biting the legs of the big dogs.

The whole lobby was a perfect pandemonium, and the din was terrific. A crowd assembled outside in the Haymarket, and asked if it was a vestry meeting; or, if not, who was being murdered, and why? Men came with poles and ropes, and tried to separate the dogs, and the police were sent for.

And in the midst of the riot that sweet young lady returned, and snatched up that sweet little dog of hers (he had laid the tyke up for a month, and had on the expression, now, of a new-born lamb) into her arms, and kissed him, and asked him if he was killed, and what those great nasty brutes of dogs had been doing to him; and he nestled up against her, and gazed up into her face with a look that seemed to say: "Oh, I'm so glad you've come to take me away from this disgraceful scene!"

She said that the people at the stores had no right to allow great savage things like those other dogs to be put with respectable people's dogs, and that she had a great mind to summon somebody.

Such is the nature of fox-terriers; and, therefore, I do not blame Montmorency for his tendency to row with cats; but he wished he had not given way to it that morning.

We were, as I have said, returning from a dip, and half-way up the High Street a cat darted out from one of the houses in front of us, and began to trot across the road. Montmorency gave a cry of joy—the cry of a stern warrior who sees his enemy given over to his hands—the sort of cry Cromwell might

have uttered when the Scots came down the hill—
and flew after his prey.

His victim was a large black tom. I never saw a
larger cat, nor a more disreputable-looking cat. It
had lost half its tail, one of its ears, and a fairly appreciable proportion of its nose. It was a long, sinewy-
looking animal. It had a calm, contented air about it.

Montmorency went for that poor cat at the rate of
twenty miles an hour; but the cat did not hurry up,
did not seem to have grasped the idea that its life was
in danger. It trotted quietly on until its would-be
assassin was within a yard of it, and then it turned
round and sat down in the middle of the road, and
looked at Montmorency with a gentle, inquiring
expression, that said:

"Yes! You want me?"

Montmorency does not lack pluck; but there was
something about the look of that cat that might have
chilled the heart of the boldest dog. He stopped
abruptly, and looked back at Tom.

Neither spoke; but the conversation that one could
imagine was clearly as follows:

The Cat: "Can I do anything for you?"

Montmorency: "No—no, thanks."

The Cat: "Don't you mind speaking, if you really
want anything, you know."

Montmorency (backing down the High Street):
"Oh no—not at all—certainly don't you trouble.

I–I am afraid I've made a mistake. I thought I knew you. Sorry I disturbed you."

The Cat: "Not at all—quite a pleasure. Sure you don't want anything, now?"

Montmorency (still backing): "Not at all, thanks—not at all—very kind of you. Good morning."

The Cat: "Good morning."

Then the cat rose, and continued his trot; and Montmorency, fitting what he calls his tail carefully into its groove, came back to us, and took up an unimportant position in the rear.

To this day, if you say the word "Cats!" to Montmorency, he will visibly shrink and look up piteously at you, as if to say:

"Please don't."

. . . It was a great success, that Irish stew. I don't think I ever enjoyed a meal more. There was something so fresh and piquant about it. One's palate gets so tired of the old hackneyed things: here was a dish with a new flavor, with a taste like nothing else on earth.

We finished up with tea and cherry tart. Montmorency had a fight with the kettle during tea-time, and came off a poor second.

Throughout the trip, he had manifested great curiosity concerning the kettle. He would sit and watch it, as it boiled, with a puzzled expression, and would try and rouse it every now and then by growling at it. When it began to splutter and steam, he regarded it as a challenge, and would want to fight it, only, at that precise moment, some one would always dash up and bear off his prey before he could get at it.

To-day he determined he would be beforehand. At the first sound the kettle made, he rose, growling, and advanced towards it in a threatening attitude. It was only a little kettle, but it was full of pluck, and it up and spit at him.

"Ah! would ye!" growled Montmorency, showing his teeth; "I'll teach ye to cheek a hard-working, respectable dog; ye miserable, long-nosed, dirty-looking scoundrel, ye. Come on!"

And he rushed at that poor little kettle, and seized it by the spout.

Then, across the evening stillness, broke a blood-curdling yelp, and Montmorency left the boat, and did a constitutional three times round the island at the rate of thirty-five miles an hour, stopping every now and then to bury his nose in a bit of cool mud.

From that day Montmorency regarded the kettle with a mixture of awe, suspicion, and hate. Whenever he saw it he would growl and back at a rapid rate, with his tail shut down, and the moment it was put upon the stove he would promptly climb out of the boat, and sit on the bank, till the whole tea business was over.

Philippa's Fox-Hunt

[E. SOMERVILLE AND MARTIN ROSS]

No one can accuse Philippa and me of having married in haste. As a matter of fact, it was but little under five years from that autumn evening on the river when I had said what is called in Ireland "the hard word," to the day in August when I was led to the altar by my best man, and was subsequently led away from it by Mrs. Sinclair Yeates. About two years out of the five had been spent by me at Shreelane in ceaseless warfare with drains, eaveshoots, chimneys, pumps; all those fundamentals, in short, that the ingenuous and improving tenant expects to find established as a basis from which to rise to higher things. As far as rising to higher things went, frequent ascents to the roof to search for leaks summed up my achievements; in fact I suffered so general a shrinkage of my ideals that the triumph of making the hall-door bell ring blinded me to the fact that the rat-holes in the hall floor were mailed up with pieces of tin biscuit boxes, and that the casual visitor could, instead of leaving a card, have easily written his name in the damp on the walls.

Philippa, however, proved adorably callous to these and similar shortcomings. She regarded Shreelane and its floundering, foundering ménage of incapables in the light of a gigantic picnic in a foreign land; she held long conversations daily with Mrs. Cadogan, in order, as she informed me, to acquire the language; without any ulterior domestic intention she engaged kitchen-maids because of the beauty of their eyes, and housemaids because they had such delightfully picturesque old mothers, and she declined to correct the phraseology of the parlor-maid, whose painful habit it was to whisper "Do ye choose cherry or clarry?" when proffering the wine. Fast-days, perhaps, afforded my wife her first insight into the sterner realities of Irish house-keeping. Philippa had what are known as High Church proclivities, and took the matter seriously.

"I don't know how we are to manage for the servants' dinner tomorrow, Sinclair," she said, coming in to my office on Thursday morning; "Julia says she 'promised God this long time that she wouldn't eat an egg on a fast-day,' and the kitchen-maid says she won't eat herrings 'without they're fried with onions,' and Mrs. Cadogan says she will 'not go to them extremes for servants.'"

"I should let Mrs. Cadogan settle the menu herself," I suggested.

"I asked her to do that," replied Philippa, "and she only said she 'thanked God *she* had no appetite!'"

The lady of the house here fell away into unseasonable laughter.

I made the demoralizing suggestion that, as we were going away for a couple of nights, we might safely leave them to fight it out, and the problem was abandoned.

Philippa had been much called on by the neighborhood in all its shades and grades, and daily she and her trousseau frocks presented themselves at hall-doors of varying dimensions in due acknowledgment of civilities. In Ireland, it may be noted, the process known in England as "summering and wintering" a new-comer does not obtain; sociability and curiosity alike forbid delay. The visit to which we owed our escape from the intricacies of the fast-day was to the Knoxes of Castle Knox, relations in some remote and tribal way of my landlord, Mr. Flurry of that ilk. It involved a short journey by train, and my wife's longest basket-trunk; it also, which was more serious, involved my being lent a horse to go out cubbing the following morning.

At Castle Knox we sank into an almost forgotten environment of draft proof windows and doors, of deep carpets, of silent servants instead of clattering belligerents. Philippa told me afterwards that it had only been by an effort that she had restrained herself from snatching up the train of her wedding-gown as she paced across the wide hall on little Sir Valentine's arm. After three weeks at Shreelane she found it difficult to remember that the floor was neither damp nor dusty.

I had the good fortune to be of the limited number of those who got on with Lady Knox, chiefly, I imagine, because I was as a worm before her, and thankfully permitted her to do all the talking.

"Your wife is extremely pretty," she pronounced autocratically, surveying Philippa between the candle-shades; "does she ride?"

Lady Knox was a short square lady, with a weather-beaten face, and an eye decisive from long habit of taking her own line across country and elsewhere. She would have made a very imposing little coachman, and would have caused her stable helpers to rue the day they had the presumption to be born; it struck me that Sir Valentine sometimes did so.

"I'm glad you like her looks," I replied, "as I fear you will find her thoroughly despicable otherwise; for one thing, she not only can't ride, but she believes that I can!"

"Oh, come, you're not as bad as all that!" my hostess was good enough to say; "I'm going to put you up on Sorcerer to-morrow, and we'll see you at the top of the hunt—if there is one. That young Knox hasn't a notion how to draw these woods."

"Well, the best run we had last year out of this place was with Flurry's hounds," struck in Miss Sally, sole daughter of Sir Valentine's house and home, from her place half-way down the table. It was not difficult to see that she and her mother held different views on the subject of Mr. Flurry Knox.

"I call it a criminal thing in any one's great-great-grandfather to rear up a preposterous troup of sons and plant them all out in his own country," Lady Knox said to me with apparent irrelevance. "I detest collaterals. Blood may be thicker than water, but it is also a great deal nastier. In this country I find that fifteenth cousins consider themselves near relations if they live within twenty miles of one!"

Having before now taken in the position with regard to Flurry Knox, I took care to accept these remarks as generalities, and turned the conversation to other themes.

"I see Mrs. Yeates is doing wonders with Mr. Hamilton," said Lady Knox presently, following the direction of my eyes, which had strayed away to where Philippa was beaming upon her left-hand neighbor, a mildewed-looking old clergyman, who was delivering a long dissertation, the purport of which we were happily unable to catch.

"She has always had a gift for the Church," I said.

"Not curates?" said Lady Knox, in her deep voice.

I made haste to reply that it was the elders of the Church who were venerated by my wife.

"Well, she has her fancy in old Eustace Hamilton; he's elderly enough!" said Lady Knox. "I wonder if she'd venerate him as much if she knew that he had fought with his sister-in-law, and they haven't spoken for thirty years! though for the matter of that," she added, "I think it shows his good sense!"

"Mrs. Knox is rather a friend of mine," I ventured.

"Is she? H'm! Well, she's not one of mine!" replied my hostess, with her usual definiteness. "I'll say one thing for her, I believe she's always been a sportswoman. She's very rich, you know, and they say she only married old Badger Knox to save his hounds from being sold to pay his debts, and then she took the horn from him and hunted them herself. Has she been rude to your wife yet? No? Oh, well, she will. It's a mere question of time. She hates all English people. You know the story they tell of her? She was coming home from London, and when she was getting her ticket the man asked if she had said a ticket for York. 'No, thank God, Cork!' says Mrs. Knox."

"Well, I rather agree with her!" said I; "but why did she fight with Mr. Hamilton?"

"Oh, nobody knows. I don't believe they know themselves! Whatever it was, the old lady drives five miles to Fortwilliam every Sunday, rather than go to his church, just outside her own back gates," Lady Knox said with a laugh like a terrier's bark. "I wish I'd fought with him myself," she said; "he gives us forty minutes every Sunday."

As I struggled into my boots the following morning, I felt that Sir Valentine's acid confidences on cub-hunting, bestowed on me at midnight, did credit to his judgment. "A very moderate amusement, my dear Major," he had said, in his dry little voice; "you should stick to shooting. No one expects you to shoot before daybreak."

It was six o'clock as I crept down-stairs, and found Lady Knox and Miss Sally at breakfast, with two lamps on the table, and a foggy daylight oozing in from under the half-raised blinds. Philippa was already in the hall, pumping up her bicycle, in a state of excitement at the prospect of her first experience of hunting that would have been more comprehensible to me had she been going to ride a strange horse, as I was. As I bolted my food I saw the horses being led past the windows, and a faint twang of a horn told that Flurry Knox and his hounds were not far off.

Miss Sally jumped up.

"If I'm not on the Cockatoo before the hounds come up, I shall never get there!" she said, hobbling out of the room in the toils of her safety habit. Her small, alert face looked very childish under her riding-hat; the lamplight struck sparks out of her thick coil of golden-red hair: I wondered how I had ever thought her like her prim little father.

She was already on her white cob when I got to the hall-door, and Flurry Knox was riding over the glistening wet grass with his hounds, while his whip, Dr. Jerome Hickey, was having a stirring time with the young entry and the rabbit-holes. They moved on without stopping, up a back avenue, under tall and dripping trees, to a thick laurel covert, at some little distance from the house. Into this the hounds were thrown, and the usual period of fidgety inaction set in for the riders, of whom, all told, there were about half-a-dozen. Lady Knox, square and solid, on her big, confidential iron-gray, was near me, and her eyes were on me and my mount; with her rubicund face and white collar she was more than ever like a coachman.

"Sorcerer looks as if he suited you well," she said, after a few minutes of silence, during which the hounds rustled and crackled steadily through the laurels; "he's a little high on the leg, and so are you, you know, so you show each other off."

Sorcerer was standing like a rock, with his good-looking head in the air and his eyes fastened on the covert. His manners, so far, had been those of a perfect gentleman, and were in marked contrast to those of Miss Sally's cob, who was sidling, hopping, and snatching unappeasably at his bit. Philippa had disappeared from view down the avenue ahead. The fog was melting, and the sun threw long blades of light through the trees; everything was quiet, and in the distance the curtained windows of the house marked the warm repose of Sir Valentine, and those of the party who shared his opinion of cubbing.

"Hark! Hark to cry there!"

It was Flurry's voice, away at the other side of the covert. The rustling and brushing through the laurels became more vehement, then passed out of hearing.

"He never will leave his hounds alone," said Lady Knox disapprovingly.

Miss Sally and the Cockatoo moved away in a series of heraldic capers toward the end of the laurel plantation, and at the same moment I saw Philippa on her bicycle shoot into view on the drive ahead of us.

"I've seen a fox!" she screamed, white with what I believe to have been personal terror, though she says it was excitement; "it passed quite close to me!"

"What way did he go?" bellowed a voice which I recognized as Dr. Hickey's, somewhere in the deep of the laurels.

"Down the drive!" returned Philippa, with a pea-hen quality in her tones with which I was quite unacquainted.

An electrifying screech of "Gone away!" was projected from the laurels by Dr. Hickey.

"Gone away!" chanted Flurry's horn at the top of the covert.

"This is what he calls cubbing!" said Lady Knox, "a mere farce!" but none the less she loosed her sedate monster into a canter.

Sorcerer got his hind-legs under him, and hardened his crest against the bit, as we all hustled along the drive after the flying figure of my wife. I knew very little about horses, but I realized that even with the hounds tumbling hysterically out of the covert, and the Cockatoo kicking the gravel into his face, Sorcerer comported himself with the manners of the best society. Up a side road I saw Flurry Knox opening half of a gate and cramming through it; in a moment we also had crammed through, and the turf of a pasture field was under our feet. Dr. Hickey leaned forward and took hold of his horse; I did likewise, with the trifling difference that my horse took hold of me, and I steered for Flurry Knox with a single-hearted purpose, the hounds, already a field ahead, being merely an exciting and noisy accompaniment of this endeavor. A heavy stone wall was the first occurrence of note. Flurry chose a place where the top was loose, and his clumsy-looking brown mare changed feet on the rattling stones like a fairy. Sorcerer came at it, tense and collected as a bow at

[274]

full stretch, and sailed steeply into the air; I saw the wall far beneath me, with an unsuspected ditch on the far side, and I felt my hat following me at the full stretch of its guard as we swept over it, then, with a long slant, we descended to earth some sixteen feet from where we had left it, and I was possessor of the gratifying fact that I had achieved a good-sized "fly," and had not perceptibly moved in my saddle. Subsequent disillusioning experience has taught me that but few horses jump like Sorcerer, so gallantly, so sympathetically, and with such supreme mastery of the subject; but none the less the enthusiasm that he imparted to me has never been extinguished, and that October morning ride revealed to me the unsuspected intoxication of fox-hunting.

Behind me I heard the scrabbling of the Cockatoo's little hoofs among the loose stones, and Lady Knox, galloping on my left, jerked a maternal chin over her shoulder to mark her daughter's progress. For my part, had there been an entire circus behind me, I was far too much occupied with ramming on my hat and trying to hold Sorcerer, to have looked round, and all my spare faculties were devoted to steering for Flurry, who had taken a right-handed turn, and was at that moment surmounting a bank of uncertain and briary aspect. I surmounted it also, with the swiftness and simplicity for which the Quaker's methods of bank-jumping had not prepared me, and two or three fields, traversed at the same steeplechase pace, brought us to a road and to an abrupt check. There, suddenly, were the hounds, scrambling in baffled silence down into the road from the opposite bank, to look for the line they had overrun, and there, amazingly, was Philippa, engaged in excited converse with several men with spades over their shoulders.

"Did ye see the fox, boys?" shouted Flurry, addressing the group.

"We did! we did!" cried my wife and her friends in chorus; "he ran up the road!"

"We'd be badly off without Mrs. Yeates!" said Flurry, as he whirled his mare round and clattered up the road with a hustle of hounds after him.

It occurred to me as forcibly as any mere earthly thing can occur to those who are wrapped in the sublimities of a run, that, for a young woman who had never before seen a fox out of a cage at the Zoo, Philippa was taking to hunting very kindly. Her cheeks were a most brilliant pink, her blue eyes shone.

"Oh, Sinclair!" she exclaimed, "they say he's going to Aussolas, and there's a road I can ride all the way!"

"Ye can, Miss! Sure we'll show you!" chorused her *cortège*.

Her foot was on the pedal ready to mount. Decidedly my wife was in no need of assistance from me.

Up the road a hound gave a yelp of discovery, and flung himself over a stile into the fields; the rest of the pack went squealing and jostling after him, and I followed Flurry over one of those infinitely varied erections, pleasantly termed "gaps" in Ireland. On this occasion the gap was made of three razor-edged slabs of slate leaning against an iron bar, and Sorcerer conveyed to me his thorough knowledge of the matter by a lift of his hind-quarters that made me feel as if I were being skillfully kicked down-stairs. To what extent I looked it, I can not say, nor providentially can Philippa, as she had already started. I only know that undeserved good luck restored to me my stirrup before Sorcerer got away with me in the next field.

What followed was, I am told, a very fast fifteen minutes; for me time was not; the empty fields rushed past uncounted, fences came and went in a flash, while the wind sang in my ears, and the dazzle of the early sun was in my eyes. I saw the hounds occasionally, sometimes pouring over a green bank, as the charging breaker lifts and flings itself, sometimes driving across a field, as the white tongues of foam slide racing over the sand; and always ahead of me was Flurry Knox, going as a man goes who knows his country, who knows his horse, and whose heart is wholly and absolutely in the right place.

Do what I would, Sorcerer's implacable stride carried me closer and closer to the brown mare, till, as I thundered down the slope of a long field, I was not twenty yards behind Flurry. Sorcerer had stiffened his neck to iron, and to slow him down was beyond me; but I fought his head away to the right, and found myself coming hard and steady at a stone-faced bank with broken ground in front of it. Flurry bore away to the left, shouting something that I did not understand. That Sorcerer shortened his stride at the right moment was entirely due to his own judgment; standing well away from the hump, he rose like a stag out of the tussocky ground, and as he swung my twelve-stone six into the air the obstacle revealed itself to him and me as consisting not of one bank but of two, and between the two lay a deep grassy lane, half choked with furze. I have often been asked to state the width of the bohereen, and can only reply that in my opinion it was at least eighteen feet; Flurry Knox and Dr. Hickey, who did not jump it, say that it is not more than five. What Sorcerer did with it, I cannot say; the sensation was of a towering flight with a kick back in it, a biggish drop, and a landing on cee-springs, still on the down-hill grade. That was how one of the best horses in Ireland took one of Ireland's most ignorant riders over a very nasty place.

A somber line of fir-wood lay ahead, rimmed with a gray wall, and in another couple of minutes we had pulled up on the Aussolas road, and were watching the hounds struggling over the wall into Aussolas demesne.

"No hurry now," said Flurry, turning in his saddle to watch the Cockatoo jump into the road; "he's to ground in the big earth inside. Well, Major, it's well for you that's a big-jumped horse. I thought you were a dead man a while ago when you faced him at the bohereen!"

I was disclaiming intention in the matter when Lady Knox and the others joined us.

"I thought you told me your wife was no sports-woman," she said to me, critically scanning Sorcerer's legs for cuts the while, "but when I saw her a minute ago she had abandoned her bicycle and was running across country like—"

"Look at her now!" interrupted Miss Sally. "Oh!—oh!" In the interval between these exclamations my incredulous eyes beheld my wife in mid-air, hand in hand with a couple of stalwart country boys, with whom she was leaping in unison from the top of a bank on to the road.

Everyone, even the saturnine Dr. Hickey, began to laugh; I rode back to Philippa, who was exchanging compliments and congratulations with her escort.

"Oh, Sinclair!" she cried, "wasn't it splendid? I saw you jumping, and everything! Where are they going now?"

"My dear girl," I said, with marital disapproval, "you're killing yourself. Where's your bicycle?

"Oh, it's punctured in a sort of lane, back there. It's all right; and then they"—she breathlessly waved her hand at her attendants—"they showed me the way."

"Begor! you proved very good, Miss!" said a grinning cavalier.

"Faith she did!" said another, polishing his shining brow with his white-flannel coat-sleeve, "she lepped like a haarse!"

"And may I ask how you propose to go home?" said I.

"I don't know and I don't care! I'm not going home!" She cast an entirely disobedient eye at me. "And your eye-glass is hanging down your back and your tie is bulging out over your waistcoat!"

The little group of riders had begun to move away.

"We're going on into Aussolas," called out Flurry; "come on, and make my grandmother give you some breakfast, Mrs. Yeates; she always has it at eight o'clock."

The front gates were close at hand, and we turned in under the tall beech-trees, with the unswept leaves rustling round the horses' feet, and the lovely blue of the October morning sky filling the spaces between smooth gray branches and golden leaves. The woods rang with the voices of the hounds, enjoying an untrammeled rabbit hunt, while the Master and the

Whip, both on foot, strolled along unconcernedly with their bridles over their arms, making themselves agreeable to my wife, an occasional touch of Flurry's horn, or a crack of Dr. Hickey's whip, just indicating to the pack that the authorities still took a friendly interest in their doings.

Down a grassy glade in the wood a party of old Mrs. Knox's young horses suddenly swept into view, headed by an old mare, who, with her tail over her back, stampeded ponderously past our cavalcade, shaking and swinging her handsome old head, while her youthful friends bucked and kicked and snapped at each other round her with the ferocious humor of their kind.

"Here, Jerome, take the horn," said Flurry to Dr. Hickey; "I'm going to see Mrs. Yeates up to the house, that way these tomfools won't gallop on top of her."

From this point it seems to me that Philippa's adventures are more worthy of record than mine, and as she has favored me with a full account of them, I venture to think my version may be relied on.

Mrs. Knox was already at breakfast when Philippa was led, quaking, into her formidable presence. My wife's acquaintance with Mrs. Knox was, so far, limited to a state visit on either side, and she found but little comfort in Flurry's assurances that his grandmother wouldn't mind if he brought all the hounds in to breakfast, coupled with the statement that she would put her eyes on sticks for the Major.

Whatever the truth of this may have been, Mrs. Knox received her guest with an equanimity quite unshaken by the fact that her boots were in the fender instead of on her feet, and that a couple of shawls of varying dimensions and degrees of age did not conceal the inner presence of a magenta flannel dressing-jacket. She installed Philippa at the table and plied her with food, oblivious as to whether the needful implements with which to eat it were forthcoming or no. She told Flurry where a vixen had reared her family, and she watched him ride away, with some biting comments on his mare's hocks screamed after him from the window.

The dining-room at Aussolas Castle is one of the many rooms in Ireland in which Cromwell is said to have stabled his horse (and probably no one would have objected less than Mrs. Knox had she been consulted in the matter). Philippa questions if the room had ever been tidied up since, and she indorses Flurry's observation that "there wasn't a day in the year you wouldn't get feeding for a hen and chickens on the floor." Opposite to Philippa, on a Louis Quinze chair, sat Mrs. Knox's wooly dog, its suspicious little eyes peering at her out of their setting of pink lids and dirty white wool. A couple of young horses outside the windows tore at the matted creepers on the walls, or thrust faces that were half-shy, half-impudent, into the room. Portly pigeons waddled to and fro on the broad window-sill, sometimes flying in to perch on the picture-frames, while they kept up incessantly a hoarse and pompous cooing.

Animals and children are, as a rule, alike destructive to conversation; but Mrs. Knox, when she chose, *bien entendu,* could have made herself agreeable in a Noah's ark, and Philippa has a gift of sympathetic attention that personal experience has taught me to regard with distrust as well as respect, while it has often made me realize the worldly wisdom of Kingsley's injunction:

Be good, sweet maid, and let who will be clever.

Family prayers, declaimed by Mrs. Knox with alarming austerity, followed close on breakfast, Philippa and a vinegar-faced henchwoman forming the family. The prayers were long, and through the open window as they progressed came distantly a whoop or two; the declamatory tones staggered a little, and then continued at a distinctly higher rate of speed.

"Ma'am! Ma'am!" whispered a small voice at the window.

Mrs. Knox made a repressive gesture and held on her way. A sudden outcry of hounds followed, and the owner of the whisper, a small boy with a face freckled like a turkey's egg, darted from the window and dragged a donkey and bath-chair into view. Philippa admits to having lost the thread of the discourse, but she thinks that the "Amen" that immediately ensued can hardly have come in its usual place. Mrs. Knox shut the book abruptly, scrambled up from her knees, and said, "They've found!"

In a surprisingly short space of time she had added to her attire her boots, a fur cape, and a garden hat, and was in the bath-chair, the small boy stimulating the donkey with the success peculiar to his class, while Philippa hung on behind.

The woods of Aussolas are hilly and extensive, and on that particular morning it seemed that they held as many foxes as hounds. In vain was the horn blown and the whips cracked, small rejoicing parties of hounds, each with a fox of its own, scoured to and fro: every laborer in the vicinity had left his work, and was sedulously heading every fox with yells that would have befitted a tiger hunt, and sticks and stones when occasion served.

"Will I pull out as far as the big rosy-dandhrum, ma'am?" inquired the small boy; "I see three of the dogs go in it, and they yowling."

E. SOMERVILLE AND MARTIN ROSS

"You will," said Mrs. Knox, thumping the donkey on the back with her umbrella; "here! Jeremiah Regan! Come down out of that with that pitchfork! Do you want to kill the fox, you fool?"

"I do not, your honor, ma'am," responded Jeremiah Regan, a tall young countryman, emerging from a bramble brake.

"Did you see him?" said Mrs. Knox eagerly.

"I seen himself and his ten pups drinking below at the lake ere yestherday, your honor, ma'am, and he as big as a chestnut horse!" said Jeremiah.

"Faugh! Yesterday!" snorted Mrs. Knox; "go on to the rhododendrons, Johnny!"

The party, reenforced by Jeremiah and the pitchfork, progressed at a high rate of speed along the shrubbery path, encountering *en route* Lady Knox, stooping on to her horse's neck under the sweeping branches of the laurels.

"Your horse is too high for my coverts, Lady Knox," said the Lady of the Manor, with a malicious eye at Lady Knox's flushed face and dinged hat; "I'm afraid you will be left behind like Absalom when the hounds go away!"

"As they never do anything here but hunt rabbits," retorted her ladyship, "I don't think that's likely."

Mrs. Knox gave her donkey another whack, and passed on.

"Rabbits, my dear!" she said scornfully to Philippa. "That's all she knows about it. I declare, it disgusts me to see a woman of that age making such a Judy of herself! Rabbits indeed!"

Down in the thicket of rhododendron everything was very quiet for a time. Philippa strained her eyes in vain to see any of the riders; the horn blowing and the whip cracking passed on almost out of hearing. Once or twice a hound worked through the rhododendrons, glanced at the party, and hurried on, immersed in business. All at once Johnny, the donkey-boy, whispered excitedly:

"Look at he! Loot at he!" and pointed to a boulder of gray rock that stood out among the dark evergreens. A big yellow cub was crouching on it; he instantly slid into the shelter of the bushes, and the irrepressible Jeremiah, uttering a rending shriek, plunged into the thicket after him. Two or three hounds came rushing at the sound, and after this Philippa says she finds some difficulty in recalling the proper order of events; chiefly, she confesses, because of the wholly ridiculous tears of excitement that blurred her eyes.

"We ran," she said, "we simply tore, and the donkey galloped, and as for that old Mrs. Knox, she was giving cracked screams to the hounds all the time, and they were screaming too; and then somehow we were all out on the road!"

What seems to have occurred was that three couple of hounds, Jeremiah Regan, and Mrs. Knox's equipage, among them somehow hustled the cub out of Aussolas demesne and up on to a hill on the farther side of the road. Jeremiah was sent back by this mistress to fetch Flurry, and the rest of the party pursued a thrilling course along the road, parallel with that of the hounds, who were hunting slowly through the gorse on the hillside.

"Upon my honor and word, Mrs. Yeates, my dear, we have the hunt to ourselves!" said Mrs. Knox to the panting Philippa, as they pounded along the road. "Johnny, d'ye see the fox?"

"I do, ma'am!" shrieked Johnny, who possessed the usual field-glass vision bestowed upon his kind. "Look at him over-right us on the hill above! Hi! The spotty dog have him! No, he's gone from him! *Givar out o' that!*" This to the donkey, with blows that sounded like the beating of carpets, and produced rather more dust.

They had left Aussolas some half a mile behind, when, from a strip of wood on their right, the fox suddenly slipped over the bank on to the road just ahead of them, ran up it for a few yards and whisked in at a small entrance gate, with the three couple of hounds yelling on a red-hot scent, not thirty yards behind. The bath-chair party whirled in at their heels, Philippa and the donkey considerably blown, Johnny scarlet through his freckles, but as fresh as paint, the old lady blind and deaf to all things save the chase. The hounds went raging through the shrubs beside the drive, and away down a grassy slope toward a shallow glen, in the bottom of which ran a little stream, and after them over the grass bumped the bath-chair. At the stream they turned sharply and ran up the glen toward the avenue, which crossed it by means of a rough stone viaduct.

"'Pon me conscience, he's into the old culvert!" exclaimed Mrs. Knox; "there was one of my hounds choked there once, long ago! Beat on the donkey, Johnny!"

At this juncture Philippa's narrative again becomes incoherent, not to say breathless. She is, however, positive that it was somewhere about here that the upset of the bath-chair occurred, but she cannot be clear as to whether she picked up the donkey or Mrs. Knox, or whether she herself was picked up by Johnny while Mrs. Knox picked up the donkey. From my knowledge of Mrs. Knox I should say she picked up herself and no one else. At all events, the next salient point is the palpitating moment when Mrs. Knox, Johnny, and Philippa successively applying an eye to the opening of the culvert by which the stream trickled under the viaduct, while five dripping hounds bayed and leaped around them, discovered by more senses than that of sight that the fox was in it, and furthermore that one of the hounds was in it, too.

"There's a sthrong grating before him at the far end," said Johnny, his head in at the mouth of the hole, his voice sounding as if he were talking into a jug, "the two of them's fighting in it; they'll be choked surely!"

"Then don't stand gabbling there, you little fool, but get in and pull the hound out!" exclaimed Mrs. Knox, who was balancing herself on a stone in the stream.

"I'd be in dread, ma'am," whined Johnny.

"Balderdash!" said the implacable Mrs. Knox. "In with you!"

I understand that Philippa assisted Johnny into the culvert, and presume it was in so doing that she acquired the two Robinson Crusoe bare footprints which decorated her jacket when I next met her.

"Have you go hold of him yet, Johnny?" cried Mrs. Knox up the culvert.

"I have, ma'am, by the tail," responded Johnny's voice, sepulchral in the depths.

"Can you stir him, Johnny?"

"I cannot, ma'am, and the wather is rising in it."

"Well, please God, they'll not open the mill dam!" remarked Mrs. Knox philosophically to Philippa, as she caught hold of Johnny's dirty ankles. "Hold on to the tail, Johnny!"

She hauled, with, as might be expected, no appreciable result. "Run, my dear, and look for somebody, and we'll have that fox yet!"

Philippa ran, whither she knew not, pursued by fearful visions of bursting mill dams, and maddened foxes at bay. As she sped up the avenue she heard voices, robust male voices, in a shrubbery, and made for them. Advancing along an embowered walk toward her was what she took for one wild instant to be a funeral; a second glance showed her that it was a party of clergymen of all ages, walking by twos and threes in the dappled shade of the over-arching trees. Obviously she had intruded her sacrilegious presence into a Clerical Meeting. She acknowledges that at this awe-inspiring spectacle she faltered, but the thought of Johnny, the hound, and the fox, suffocating, possibly drowning together in the culvert, nerved her. She does not remember what she said or how she said it, but I fancy she must have conveyed to them the impression that old Mrs. Knox was being drowned, as she immediately found herself heading a charge of the Irish Church toward the scene of disaster.

Fate has not always used me well, but on this occasion it was mercifully decreed that I and the other members of the hunt should be privileged to arrive in time to see my wife and her rescue party precipitating themselves down the glen.

"Holy Biddy!" ejaculated Flurry, "is she running a paper-chase with all the parsons? But look! For pity's sake will you look at my grandmother and my Uncle Eustace?"

Mrs. Knox and her sworn enemy the old clergy-man, whom I had met at dinner the night before, were standing, apparently in the stream, tugging at two bare legs that projected from a hole in the viaduct, and arguing at the top of their voices. The bath-chair lay on its side with the donkey grazing beside it, on the bank a stout Archdeacon was tendering advice, and the hounds danced and howled round the entire group.

"I tell you, Eliza, you had better let the Archdeacon try," thundered Mr. Hamilton.

"Then I tell you I will not!" vociferated Mrs. Knox, with a tug at the end of the sentence that elicited a subterranean lament from Johnny. "Now who was right about the second grating? I told you so twenty years ago!"

Exactly as Philippa and her rescue party arrived, the efforts of Mrs. Knox and her brother-in-law triumphed. The struggling, sopping form of Johnny was slowly drawn from the hole, drenched, speechless, but clinging to the stern of a hound, who, in its turn, had its jaws fast in the hindquarters of a limp, yellow cub.

"Oh, it's dead!" wailed Philippa, "I *did* think I should have been in time to save it!"

"Well, if that doesn't beat all!" said Dr. Hickey.

Bob, Son of Battle

[ALFRED OLLIVANT]

I

The sun was hiding behind the Pike. Over the lowlands the feathery breath of night hovered still. And the hillside was shivering in the chillness of dawn.

Down on the silvery sward beside the Stony Bottom there lay the ruffled body of a dead sheep. All about the victim the dewy ground was dark and patchy like disheveled velvet; bracken trampled down; stones displaced as though by straggling feet; and the whole spotted with the all-pervading red.

A score yards up the hill, in a writhing confusion of red and gray, two dogs at death-grips. While yet higher, a pack of wild-eyed hill-sheep watched, fascinated, the bloody drama.

The fight raged. Red and gray, blood-spattered, murderous-eyed; the crimson froth dripping from their jaws; now rearing high with arching crests and wrestling paws; now rolling over in tumbling, tossing, worrying disorder—the two fought out their blood-feud.

Above, the close-packed flock huddled and stamped, ever edging nearer to watch the issue. Just so must the women of Rome have craned round the arenas to see two men striving in death-struggle.

The first cold flicker of dawn stole across the green. The red eye of the morning peered aghast over the shoulder of the Pike. And from the sleeping dale there arose the yodling of a man driving his cattle home.

Day was upon them.

James Moore was waked by a little whimpering cry beneath his window. He leapt out of bed and rushed to look; for well he knew 'twas not for nothing that the old dog was calling.

"Lord o' mercy! whativer's come to yo', Owd Un?" he cried in anguish. And, indeed, his favourite, wardaubed almost past recognition, presented a pitiful spectacle.

In a moment the Master was downstairs and out, examining him.

"Poor old lad, yo' have caught it this time!" he

cried. There was a ragged tear on the dog's cheek; a deep gash in his throat from which the blood still welled, staining the white escutcheon on his chest; while head and neck were clotted with the red.

Hastily the Master summoned Maggie. After her, Andrew came hurrying down. And a little later a tiny, night-clad, naked-footed figure appeared in the door, wide-eyed, and then fled, screaming.

They doctored the old warrior on the table in the kitchen. Maggie tenderly washed his wounds and dressed them with gentle, pitying fingers; and he stood all the while grateful yet fidgeting, looking up into his master's face as if imploring to be gone.

"He mun a had a rare tussle wi' some one—eh, dad?" said the girl, as she worked.

"Ay; and wi' whom? 'Twasn't for nowt he got fightin', I war'nt. Nay; he's a tale to tell, has Th' Owd Un, and—Ah-h-h! I thowt as much. Look 'ee!" For bathing the bloody jaws, he had come upon a cluster of tawny red hair, hiding in the corners of the lips.

The secret was out. Those few hairs told their own accusing tale. To but one creature in the Daleland could they belong—"The Tailless Tyke."

"He mun a bin trespassin'!" cried Andrew.

"Ay, and up to some o' his bloody work, I'll lay my life," the Master answered. "But Th' Owd Un shall show us."

The old dog's hurts proved less severe than had at first seemed possible. His good gray coat, forest-thick about his throat, had never served him in such good stead. And at length, the wounds washed and sewn up, he jumped down all in a hurry from the table and made for the door.

"Noo, owd lad, yo' may show us," said the Master, and, with Andrew, hurried after him down the hill, along the stream, and over Langholm How. And as they neared the Stony Bottom, the sheep, herding in groups, raised frightened heads to stare.

Of a sudden a cloud of poisonous flies rose, buzzing, up before them; and there in a dimple of the ground lay a murdered sheep. Deserted by its comrades, the glazed eyes staring helplessly upward, the throat horribly worried, it slept its last sleep.

The matter was plain to see. At last the Black Killer had visited Kenmuir.

"I guessed as much," said the Master, standing over the mangled body. "Well, it's the worst night's work ever the Killer done. I reck'n Th'Owd Un come on him while he was at it; and then they fought. And, ma word *it* mun ha' ben a fight too." For all around were traces of that terrible struggle: the earth torn up and tossed, bracken uprooted, and throughout little dabs of wool and tufts of tawny hair, mingling with dark-stained iron-gray wisps.

James Moore walked slowly over the battlefield, stooping down as though he were gleaning. And gleaning he was.

A long time he bent so, and at length raised himself.

"The Killer has killed his last," he muttered; "Red Wull has run his course." Then, turning to Andrew: "Run yo' home, lad, and fetch the men to carry yon away," pointing to the carcass. "And Bob, lad, yo've done your work for to-day, and right well too; go yo' home wi' him. I'm off to see to this!"

He turned and crossed the Stony Bottom. His face was set like a rock. At length the proof was in his hand. Once and for all the hill-country should be rid of its scourge.

As he stalked up the hill, a dark head appeared at his knee. Two big gray eyes, half doubting, half penitent, wholly wistful, looked up at him, and a silvery brush signalled a mute request.

"Eh, Owd Un, but yo' should ha' gone wi' Andrew," the Master said. "Hooiver, as yo' are here, come along." And he strode away up the hill, gaunt and menacing, with the gray dog at his heels.

As they approached the house, M'Adam was standing in the door, sucking his eternal twig. James Moore eyed him closely as he came, but the sour face framed in the door betrayed nothing. Sarcasm, surprise, challenge, were all writ there, plain to read; but no guilty consciousness of the other's errand, no storm of passion to hide a failing heart. If it was acting it was splendidly done.

As man and dog passed through the gap in the hedge, the expression of the little man's face changed again. He started forward.

"James Moore, as I live!" he cried, and advanced with both hands extended, as though welcoming a long-lost brother. "Deed and it's a weary while sin' ye've honoured ma puir hoose." And, in fact, it was nigh twenty years. "I tak'it gey kind in ye to look in on a lonely auld man. Come ben and let's ha'a crack. James Moore kens weel hoo welcome he aye is in ma bit biggin'."

The Master ignored the greeting.

"One o' ma sheep been killed back o' t' Dyke," he announced shortly, jerking his thumb over his shoulder.

"The Killer?"

"The Killer."

The cordiality beaming in every wrinkle of the little man's face was absorbed in a wondering interest: and that again gave place to sorrowful sympathy.

"Dear, dear! it's come to that, has it—at last?" he said gently, and his eyes wandered to the gray dog and dwelt mournfully upon him. "Man, I'm sorry —I canna tell ye I'm surprised. Masel', I kent it all

alang. But gin Adam M'Adam had tell't, ye'd no ha'
believed him. Weel, weel, he's lived his life, gin ony
dog iver did; and noo he maun gang where he's sent
a many before him. Puir mon! puir tyke!" He
heaved a sigh, profoundly melancholy, tenderly sympathetic. Then, brightening up a little: "Ye'll ha'
come for the gun?"

James Moore listened to his harangue at first puzzled. Then he caught the other's meaning, and his
eyes flashed.

"Ye fool, M'Adam! Did ye hear iver tell o' a
sheep-dog worryin' his master's sheep?"

The little man was smiling and suave again now,
rubbing his hands softly together.

"Ye're right, I never did. But your dog is not as ither
dogs—'There's none like him—none,' I've heard ye
say so yersel, mony a time. An' I'm wi' ye. There's
none like him—for devilment." His voice began to
quiver and his face to blaze. "It's his cursed cunning
that's deceived ivery one but me—whelp o' Satan that
he is!" He shouldered up to his tall adversary. "If not
him, wha else had done it?" he asked, looking up into
the other's face as if daring him to speak.

The Master's shaggy eyebrows lowered. He tow-
ered above the other like the Muir Pike above its
surrounding hills.

"Wha, ye ask?" he replied coldly, "and I answer
you. Your Red Wull, M'Adam, your Red Wull. It's

your Wull's the Black Killer! It's your Wull's bin the plague o' the land these months past! It's your Wull's killed ma sheep back o' yon!"

At that all the little man's affected good-humour fled.

"Ye lee, mon! ye lee!" he cried in a dreadful scream, dancing up to his antagonist. "I knoo hoo 'twad be. I said so. I see what ye're at. Ye've found at last—blind that ye've been!—that it's yer ain hell's tyke that's the Killer; and noo ye think by yer leein' impitations to throw the blame on ma Wullie. Ye rob me o' ma Cup, ye rob me o' ma son, ye wrang me in ilka thing; there's but ae thing left me—Wullie. And noo ye're set on takin' him awa'. But ye shall not— I'll kill ye first!"

He was all a-shake, bobbing up and down like a stopper in a soda-water bottle, and almost sobbing.

"Ha' ye no wranged me enough wi' oot that? Ye lang-leggit liar, wi' yer skulkin murderin' tyke!" he cried. "Ye say it's Wullie. Where's yer proof?"—and he snapped his fingers in the other's face.

The Master was now as calm as his foe was passionate. "Where?" he replied sternly; "why, there!" holding out his right hand. "Yon's proof enough to hang a hunner'd." For lying in his broad palm was a little bundle of that damning red hair.

"Where?"

"There!"

"Let's see it!" The little man bent to look closer.

"There's for yer proof!" he cried, and spat deliberately down into the other's naked palm. Then he stood back, facing his enemy in a manner to have done credit to a nobler deed.

James Moore strode forward. It looked as if he was about to make an end of his miserable adversary, so strongly was he moved. His chest heaved, and the blue eyes blazed. But just as one had thought to see him take his foe in the hollow of his hand and crush him, who should come stalking round the corner of the house but the Tailless Tyke.

A droll spectacle he made, laughable even at that moment. He limped sorely, his head and neck were swathed in bandages, and beneath their ragged fringe the little eyes gleamed out fiery and bloodshot.

Round the corner he came, unaware of strangers; then straightway recognizing his visitors, halted abruptly. His hackles ran up, each individual hair stood on end till his whole body resembled a new-shorn wheat-field; and a snarl, like a rusty brake shoved hard down, escaped from between his teeth. Then he trotted heavily forward, his head sinking low and lower as he came.

And Owd Bob, eager to take up the gage of battle, advanced, glad and gallant, to meet him. Daintily he picked his way across the yard, head and tail erect, perfectly self-contained. Only the long gray hair about his neck stood up like the ruff of a lady of the court of Queen Elizabeth.

But the war-worn warriors were not to be allowed their will.

"Wullie, Wullie, wad ye!" cried the little man.

"Bob, lad, coom in!" called the other. Then he turned and looked down at the man beside him, contempt flaunting in every feature.

"Well?" he said shortly.

M'Adam's hands were opening and shutting; his face was quite white beneath the tan; but he spoke calmly.

"I'll tell ye the whole story, and it's the truth," he said slowly. "I was up there the morn"—pointing to the window above—"and I see Wullie crouchin' down alangside the Stony Bottom. (Ye ken he has the run o ma land o' neets, the same as your dog.) In a minnit I see anither dog squatterin' alang on your side the Bottom. He creeps up to the sheep on th' hillside, chases 'em, and doons one. The sun was risen by then, and I see the dog clear as I see you noo. It was that dog there—I swear it!" His voice rose as he spoke, and he pointed an accusing finger at Owd Bob.

"Noo, Wullie! thinks I. And afore ye could clap yer hands, Wullie was over the Bottom and on to him as he gorged—the bloody-minded murderer! They fought and fought—I could hear the roarin' a't where I stood. I watched till I could watch nae langer, and, all in a sweat, I rin doon the stairs and oot. When I got there, there was yer tyke makin' fu' split for Kenmuir, and Wullie comin' up the hill to me. It's God's truth, I'm tellin' ye. Tak' him hame, James Moore, and let his dinner be an ounce o' lead. 'Twill be the best day's work iver ye done."

The little man must be lying—lying palpably. Yet he spoke with an earnestness, a seeming belief in his own story, that might have convinced one who knew him less well. But the Master only looked down on him with a great scorn.

"It's Monday to-day," he said coldly. "I gie yo' till Saturday. If yo've not done your duty by then—and well you know what 'tis—I shall come do it for ye. Ony gate, I shall come and see. I'll remind ye agin o' Thursday—yo'll be at the Manor dinner, I suppose. Noo I've warned yo,' and you know best whether I'm in earnest or no. Boy, lad!"

He turned away, but turned again.

"I'm sorry for ye, but I've ma duty to do—so've you. Till Saturday I shall breathe no word to ony soul o' this business, so that if you see good to put him oot o' the way wi'oot bother, no one need iver know as hoo Adam M'Adam's Red Wull was the Black Killer."

He turned away for the second time. But the little man sprang after him, and clutched him by the arm.

"Look ye here, James Moore!" he cried in thick, shaky horrible voice. "Ye're big, I'm sma'; ye're strang, I'm weak; ye've ivery one to your back, I've niver a one; you tell your story, and they'll believe ye—for you gae to church; I'll tell mine, and they'll think I lie—for I dinna. But a word in your ear! If iver agin I catch ye on ma land, by—!"—he swore a great oath—"I'll no spare ye. You ken best if I'm in earnest or no." And his face was dreadful to see in its hideous determinedness.

II

That night a vague story was whispered in the Sylvester Arms. But Tammas, on being interrogated, pursed his lips and said: "Nay, I'm sworn to say nowt." Which was the old man's way of putting that he knew nowt.

On Thursday morning, James Moore and Andrew came down arrayed in all their best. It was the day of the squire's annual dinner to his tenants.

The two, however, were not allowed to start upon their way until they had undergone a critical inspection by Maggie; for the girl liked her mankind to do honour to Kenmuir on these occasions. So she brushed up Andrew, tied his scarf, saw his boots and hands were clean, and titivated him generally till she had converted the ungainly hobbledehoy into a thoroughly "likely young mon."

And all the while she was thinking of that other boy for whom on such gala days she had been wont to perform like offices. And her father, marking the tears in her eyes, and mindful of the squire's mysterious hint, said gently:

"Cheer up, lass. Happen I'll ha' news for you the night!"

The girl nodded, and smiled wanly.

"Happen so, dad," she said. But in her heart she doubted.

Nevertheless it was with a cheerful countenance that, a little later, she stood in the door with wee Anne and Owd Bob and waved the travellers Godspeed; while the golden-haired lassie, fiercely gripping the old dog's tail with one hand and her sister with the other, screamed them a wordless farewell.

The sun had reached its highest when the two wayfarers passed through the gray portals of the Manor.

In the stately entrance hall, imposing with all the evidences of a long and honourable line, were gathered now the many tenants throughout the wide March Mere Estate. Weather-beaten, rent-paying sons of the soil; most of them native-born, many of them like James Moore, whose fathers had for generations owned and farmed the land they now leased at the hands of the Sylvesters—there in the old hall they were assembled, a mighty host. And apart from the others, standing as though in irony beneath the frown of one of those steel-clad warriors who held the door, was little M'Adam, puny always, paltry-now, mocking his manhood.

The door at the far end of the hall opened, and the squire entered, beaming on everyone.

"Here you are—eh, eh! How are you all? Glad to see ye! Good-day, James! Good-day, Saunderson! Good-day to you all! Bringin' a friend with me— eh, eh!" and he stood aside to let by his agent, Parson Leggy, and last of all, shy and blushing, a fair-haired young giant.

"If it bain't David!" was the cry. "Eh, lad, we's fain to see yo'! And yo'm lookin' stout, surely!" And they thronged about the boy, shaking him by the hand, and asking him his story.

'Twas but a simple tale. After his flight on the eventful night he had gone south, drovering. He had written to Maggie, and been surprised and hurt to receive no reply. In vain he had waited, and too proud to write again, had remained ignorant of his father's recovery, neither caring nor daring to return. Then by mere chance, he had met the squire at the York cattle-show; and that kind man, who knew his story, had eased his fears and obtained from him a promise to return as soon as the term of his engagement had expired. And there he was.

The Dalesmen gathered round the boy, listening to his tale, and in return telling him the home news, and chaffing him about Maggie.

Of all the people present, only one seemed unmoved, and that was M'Adam. When first David had entered he had started forward, a flush of colour warming his thin cheeks; but no one had noticed his emotion; and now, back again beneath his armour, he watched the scene, a sour smile playing about his lips.

"I think the lad might ha' the grace to come and say he's sorry for 'temptin' to murder me. Hooiver"—with a characteristic shrug—"I suppose I'm onraisonable."

Then the gong rang out its summons, and the squire led the way into the great dining-hall. At the one end of the long table, heavy with all the solid delicacies of such a feast, he took his seat with the master of Kenmuir upon his right. At the other end was Parson Leggy. While down the sides the stalwart Dalesmen were arrayed, with M'Adam a little lost figure in the centre.

At first they talked but little, awed like children: knives plied, glasses tinkled, the carvers had all their work, only the tongues were at rest. But the squire's ringing laugh and the parson's cheery tones soon put them at their ease; and a babel of voices rose and waxed.

Of them all, only M'Adam sat silent. He talked to no man, and you may be sure no one talked to him. His hand crept oftener to his glass than plate, till the sallow face began to flush, and the dim eyes to grow unnaturally bright.

Toward the end of the meal there was loud tapping on the table, calls for silence, and men pushed back their chairs. The squire was on his feet to make his annual speech.

He started by telling them how glad he was to see them there. He made an allusion to Owd Bob and the Shepherds' Trophy which was heartily applauded. He touched on the Black Killer, and said he had a remedy to propose: that Th' Owd Un should be set upon the criminal's track—a suggestion which was received with enthusiasm, while M'Adam's cackling laugh could be heard high above the rest.

From that he dwelt upon the existing condition of agriculture, the depression in which he attributed to the late Radical Government. He said that now with the Conservatives in office, and a ministry composed of "honourable men and gentlemen" he felt convinced that things would brighten. The Radicals' one ambition was to set class against class, landlord against tenant. Well, during the last five hundred years, the Sylvesters had rarely been—he was sorry to have to confess it—good men [laughter and dissent]; but he never yet heard of the

Sylvester—though he shouldn't say it—who was a bad landlord [loud applause].

This was a free country, and any tenant of his who was not content [a voice, "'Oo says we bain't?"]—"thank you, thank you!"—well, there was room for him outside. [Cheers.] He thanked God from the bottom of his heart that during the forty years he had been responsible for the March Mere Estate, there had never been any friction between him and his people [cheers], and he didn't think there ever would be [Loud cheers.]

"Thank you, thank you!" And his motto was "Shun a Radical as you do the devil!"—and he was very glad to see them all there—very glad; and he wished to give them a toast, "The Queen! God bless her!" and—wait a minute!—with her Majesty's name to couple—he was sure that gracious lady would wish it—that of "Owd Bob o' Kenmuir!" then he sat down abruptly amid thundering applause.

The toasts duly honoured, James Moore, by prescriptive right as Master of Kenmuir, rose to answer.

He began by saying that he spoke "as representing all the tenants,"—but he was interrupted.

"Na," came a shrill voice from half-way down the table. "Ye'll except me, James Moore. I'd as lief be represented by Judas!"

There were cries of "Hold ye gab, little mon!" and the squire's voice, "That'll do, Mr. M'Adam!"

The little man restrained his tongue, but his eyes gleamed like a ferret's; and the Master continued his speech.

He spoke briefly and to the point, in short phrases. And all the while M'Adam kept up a low-voiced, running commentary. At length he could control himself no longer. Half rising from his chair, he leant forward with hot face and burning eyes, and cried: "Sit doon, James Moore! Hoo daur ye stan' there like an honest man, ye whitewashed sepulchre? Sit doon, I say, or"—threateningly—"wad ye hae me come to ye?"

At that the Dalesmen laughed uproariously, and even the Master's grim face relaxed. But the squire's voice rang out sharp and stern.

"Keep silence and sit down, Mr. M'Adam! D'you hear me sir? If I have to speak to you again it will be to order you to leave the room."

The little man obeyed, sullen and vengeful, like a beaten cat.

The Master concluded his speech by calling on all present to give three cheers for the squire, her ladyship, and the young ladies.

The call was responded to enthusiastically, every man standing. Just as the noise was at its zenith, Lady Eleanour herself, with her two fair daughters, glided into the gallery at the end of the hall; whereat the cheering became deafening.

Slowly the clamour subsided. One by one the tenants sat down. At length there was left standing only
one solitary figure—M'Adam.

His face was set, and he gripped the chair in front
of him with thin, nervous hands.

"Mr. Sylvester," he began in low yet clear voice,
"ye said this is a free country and we're a' free men.
And that bein' so, I'll tak' the liberty, wi' yer permission, to say a word. It's maybe the last time I'll be
wi' ye, so I hope ye'll listen to me."

The Dalesmen looked surprised, and the squire
uneasy. Nevertheless he nodded assent.

The little man straightened himself. His face was
tense as though strung up to a high resolve. All the
passion had fled from it, all the bitterness was gone;
and left behind was a strange ennobling earnestness.
Standing there in the silence of that great hall, with
every eye upon him, he looked like some prisoner at
the bar about to plead for his life.

"Gentlemen," he began, "I've bin amang ye noo
a score years, and I can truly say there's not a man
in this room I can ca' 'Friend,'" He looked along
the ranks of upturned faces. "Ay, David, I see ye,
and you, Mr. Hornbut, and you, Mr. Sylvester—
ilka one o' you, and not one as'd back me like a
comrade gin a trouble came upon me." There was
no rebuke in the grave little voice—it merely stated
a hard fact.

"There's I doot no one amang ye but has some one—friend or blood—wham he can turn to when things are sair wi' him. I've no one.

"I bear alane my lade o' care'—

alane wi' Wullie, who stands to me, blaw or snaw, rain or shine. And whiles I'm feared he'll be took from me." He spoke this last half to himself, a grieved, puzzled expression on his face, as though lately he had dreamed some ill dream.

"Forbye, Wullie, I've no friend on God's earth. And, mind ye, a bad man aften mak's a good friend—but ye've never given me the chance. It's a sair thing that, gentlemen, to ha' to fight the battle o' life alane: no one to pat ye on th' back, no one to say 'Weel done.' It hardly gies a man a chance. For gin he does try and yet fails, men never mind the tryin', they only mark the failin'.

"I dinna blame ye. There's something bred in me, it seems, as set ivery one agin me. It's the same wi' Wullie and the tykes—they're doon on him same as men are on me. I suppose we was made so. Sin' I was a lad it's aye bin the same. From school days I've had ivery one agin me.

"In ma life I've had three friends. Ma mither—and she went; then ma wife"—he gave a great swallow—"and she's awa'; and I may say they're the only two

human bein's as ha' lived on God's earth in ma time
that iver tied to bear wi' me;—and Wullie. A man's
mither—a man's wife—a man's dog! it's aften a' he has
in this warld; and the more he prizes them the more
like they are to be took from him." The little earnest
voice shook, and the dim eyes puckered and filled.

"Sin I've bin amang ye—twenty-odd years—can
any man here mind speakin' any word that wasna ill
to me?" He paused; there was no reply.

"I'll tell ye. All the time I've lived here I've had
one kindly word spoke to me, and that a fortnight
gone, and not by a man then—by her ladyship. God
bless her!" He glanced up into the gallery. There was
no one visible there; but a curtain at one end shook
as though it were sobbing.

"Weel, I'm thinkin' we'll be gaein' in a wee while
noo, Wullie and me, alane and thegither, as we've aye
done. And it's time we went. Ye've had enough o'
us, and it's no for me to blame ye. And when I'm
gone what'll ye say o' me? 'He was a drunkard.' I
am. 'He was a sinner.' I am. "He was ilka thing he
shouldna be.' I am. 'We're glad he's gone.' That's
what ye'll say o' me. And it's but ma deserts."

The gentle, condemning voice ceased, and began
again.

"That's what I am. Gin things had been differ', aiblins I'd ha' bin differ'. D'ye ken Robbie Burns? That's
a man I've read, and read, and read. D'ye ken why I

love him as some o' you do yer Bibles? Because there's
a humanity about him. A weak man hissel', aye slippin', slippin', and tryin' to haud up; sorrowin' ae
minute, sinnin' the next; doin' ill deeds and wishin'
'em undone—just a plain human man, a sinner. And
that's why I'm thinkin' he's tender for us as is like
him. *He understood.* It's what he wrote—after ain o'
his tumbles. I'm thinkin'—that I was goin' to tell ye:

'Then gently scan yer brother man,

Still gentler sister woman,

Though they may gang a kennin' wrang,

To step aside is human'—

the doctrine o' Charity. Gie him his chance, says
Robbie, though he be a sinner. Mony a mon'd be
differ', mony bad'd be gude, gin they had but their
chance. Gie 'em their chance, says he; and I'm wi'
him. As 'tis, ye see me here—a bad man wi' a streak
o' good in him. Gin I'd had ma chance, aiblins 'twad
be—a good man wi' just a spice o' the devil in him.
A' the differ' betune what is and what might ha' bin."

III

He sat down. In the great hall there was silence, save
for a tiny sound from the gallery like a sob suppressed.

The squire rose hurriedly and left the room.

After him, one by one, trailed the tenants.

At length, two only remained—M'Adam, sitting solitary with a long array of empty chairs on either hand; and, at the far end of the table, Parson Leggy, stern, upright, motionless.

When the last man had left the room the parson rose and with lips tight-set strode across the silent hall.

"M'Adam," he said rapidly and almost roughly, "I've listened to what you've said, as I think we all have, with a sore heart. You hit hard—but I think you were right. And if I've not done my duty by you as I ought—and I fear I've not—it's now my duty as God's minister to be the first to say I'm sorry." And it was evident from his face what an effort the words cost him.

The little man tilted back his chair, and raised his head.

It was the old M'Adam who looked up. The thin lips were curled; a grin was crawling across the mocking face; and he wagged his head gently, as he looked at the speaker through the slits of his half-closed eyes.

"Mr. Hornbut, I believe ye thocht me in earnest, 'deed and I do!" He leaned back in his chair and laughed softly. "Ye swallered it all down like best butter. Dear, dear! to think o' that!" Then, stretching forward: "Mr. Hornbut, I was playin' wi' ye."

The parson's face, as he listened, was ugly to watch. He shot out a hand and grabbed the scoffer by his coat; then dropped it again and turned abruptly away.

As he passed through the door a little sneering voice called after him:

"Mr. Hornbut, I ask ye hoo you, a minister o' the Church of England, can reconcile it to yer conscience to think—though it be but for a minute—that there can be ony good in a man and him no churchgoer? Sir, ye're a heretic—not to say a heathen!" He sniggered to himself, and his hand crept to a half-emptied wine decanter.

An hour later, James Moore, his business with the squire completed, passed through the hall on his way out. Its only occupant was now M'Adam, and the Master walked straight up to his enemy.

"M'Adam," he said gruffly, holding out a sinewy hand, "I'd like to say—"

The little man knocked aside the token of friendship.

"Na, na. No cant, if ye please, James Moore. That'll aiblins go doon wi' the parsons, but not wi' me. I ken you and you ken me, and all the whitewash i' th' warld 'll no deceive us."

The Master turned away, and his face was hard as the nether millstone. But the little man pursued him.

"I was nigh forgettin'," he said. "I've a surprise for ye, James Moore. But I hear it's yer birthday on Sunday, and I'll keep it till then—he! he!"

"Ye'll see me before Sunday, M'Adam," the other answered. "On Saturday, as I told yo', I'm comin' to see if yo've done yer duty."

"Whether ye come, James Moore, is your business. Whether ye'll iver go, once there, I'll mak' mine. I've warned ye twice noo"—and the little man laughed that harsh, cackling laugh of his.

At the door of the hall the Master met David.

"Noo lad, yo're comin' along wi' Andrew and me," he said; "Maggie'll niver forgie us if we dinna bring yo' home wi' us."

"Thank you kindly, Mr. Moore," the boy replied. "I've to see squire first; and then yo' may be sure I'll be after you."

The Master faltered a moment.

"David, ha'n yo' spoke to yer father yet?" he asked in low voice. "Yo' should lad."

The boy made a gesture of dissent.

"I canna," he said petulantly.

"I would, lad," the other advised. "An yo' don't yo' may be sorry after."

As he turned away he heard the boy's steps, dull and sodden, as he crossed the hall; and then a thin, would-be cordial voice in the emptiness:

"I declar' if 'tisna David! The return o' the Prodeegal—he! he! So ye've seen yer auld dad at last, and the last; the proper place, say ye, for yer father—he! he! Eh, lad, but I'm blithe to see ye. D'ye mind when we was last thegither? Ye was kneelin' on ma chest: 'Your time's come, dad,' says you, and wangs me o'er the face—he! he! I mind it as if 'twas yesterday. Weel, weel, we'll say nae mair about it. Boys will be boys. Sons will be sons. Accidents will happen. And if at first ye don't succeed, why, try, try again—he! he!"

Dusk was merging into darkness when the Master and Andrew reached the Dalesman's Daughter. It had been long dark when they emerged from the cosy parlour of the inn and plunged out into the night.

As they crossed the Silver Lea and trudged over that familiar ground, where a fortnight since had been fought out the battle of the Cup, the wind fluttered past them in spasmodic gasps.

"There's trouble in the wind," said the Master.

"Ay," answered his laconic son.

All day there had been no breath of air, and the sky dangerously blue. But now a world of black was surging up from the horizon, smothering the star-lit night; and small dark clouds, like puffs of smoke, detaching themselves from the main body, were driving tempestuously forward—the vanguard of the storm.

In the distance was a low rumbling like heavy tumbrils on the floor of heaven. All about, the wind sounded hollow like a mighty scythe on corn. The air was oppressed with a leaden blackness—no glimmer of light on any hand; and as they began the ascent of the Pass they reached out blind hands to feel along the rock-face.

A sea-fret, cool and wetting, fell. A few big rain-drops splashed heavily down. The wind rose with a leap and roared past them up the rocky track. And the water-gates of heaven were flung wide.

Wet and weary, they battled on; thinking some-times of the cosy parlour behind; sometimes of the home in front; wondering whether Maggie, in flat contradiction of her father's orders, would be up to welcome them; or whether Owd Bob would come out to meet them.

The wind volleyed past them like salvoes of artillery. The rain stormed at them from above; spat at them from the rock-face; and leapt up at them from their feet.

Once they halted for a moment, finding a miser-able shelter in a crevice of the rock.

"It's a Black Killer's night," panted the Master. "I reck'n he's oot."

"Ay," the boy gasped, "reck'n he is."

Up and up they climbed through the blackness, blind and buffeted. The eternal thunder of the rain was all about them; the clamour of the gale above; and far beneath, the roar of angry waters.

Once, in a lull in the storm, the Master turned and looked back into the blackness along the path they had come.

"Did ye hear onythin'?" he roared above the muf-fled soughing of the wind.

"Nay!" Andrew shouted back.

"I thowt I heard a step!" the Master cried, peering down. But nothing could he see.

Then the wind leaped to life again like a giant from his sleep, drowning all sound with its hurricane voice; and they turned and bent to their task again.

Nearing the summit, the Master turned once more.

"There it was again!" he called; but his words were swept away on the storm; and they buckled to the struggle afresh.

Ever and anon the moon gleamed down through the riot of tossing sky. Then they could see the wet wall above them, with the water tumbling down its sheer face; and far below, in the roaring gutter of the Pass a brown-stained torrent. Hardly, however, had they time to glance around when a mass of cloud would hurry jealously up, and all again was blackness and noise.

At length, nigh spent, they topped the last and steepest pitch of the Pass, and emerged into the Devil's Bowl. There, overcome with their exertions, they flung themselves on to the soaking ground to draw breath.

Behind them, the wind rushed with a sullen roar up the funnel of the Pass. It screamed above them as though ten million devils were a-horse; and blurted out on to the wild Marches beyond.

As they lay there, still panting, the moon gleamed down in momentary graciousness. In front, through the lashing rain, they could discern the hillocks that squat, hag-like, round the Devil's Bowl; and lying in its bosom, its white waters, usually so still, ploughed now into a thousand furrows, the Lone Tarn.

The Master raised his head and craned forward at the ghostly scene. Of a sudden he reared himself on to his arms, and stayed motionless awhile. Then he dropped as though dead, forcing down Andrew with an iron hand.

"Lad, did'st see?" he whispered.

"Nay: what was't?" the boy replied, roused by his father's tone.

"There!"

But as the Master pointed forward, a blue of cloud intervened and all was dark. Quickly it passed; and again the lantern of the night shone down. And Andrew, looking with all his eyes, saw indeed.

There, in front, by the fretting waters of the Tarn, packed in a solid phalanx, with every head turned in the same direction, was a flock of sheep. They were motionless, all-intent, staring with horror-bulging eyes. A column of steam rose from their bodies into the rain-pierced air. Panting and palpitating, yet they stood with their backs to the water, as though determined to sell their lives dearly. Beyond them, not fifty yards away, crouched a hump-backed boulder, casting a long misshapen shadow in the moonlight. And beneath it were two black objects, one struggling feebly.

"The Killer!" gasped the boy, and, all ablaze with excitement, began forging forward.

"Steady, lad, steady!" urged his father, dropping a restraining hand on the boy's shoulder.

Above them a huddle of clouds flung in furious rout across the night, and the moon was veiled.

"Follow, lad!" ordered the Master, and began to crawl silently forward. As stealthily Andrew pursued. And over the sodden ground they crept, one behind the other, like two night-hawks on some foul errand.

On they crawled, lying prone during the blinks of moon, stealing forward in the dark; till, at length, the swish of the rain on the waters of the Tarn, and the sobbing of the flock in front, warned them they were near.

They skirted the trembling pack, passing so close as to brush against the flanking sheep; and yet unnoticed, for the sheep were soul-absorbed in the tragedy in front. Only, when the moon was in, Andrew could hear them huddling and stamping in the darkness. And again, as it shone out, fearfully they edged closer to watch the bloody play.

Along the Tarn edge the two crept. And still the gracious moon hid their approach, and the drunken wind drowned with its revelry the sound of their coming.

So they stole on, on hands and knees, with hearts aghast and fluttering breath; until, of a sudden, in a lull of wind, they could hear, right before them, the smack and slobber of bloody lips, chewing their bloody meal.

"Say thy prayers, Red Wull. Thy last minute's come!" muttered the Master, rising to his knees. Then, in Andrew's ear: "When I rush, lad, follow!" For he thought when the moon rose, to jump in on the great dog, and, surprising him as he lay gorged and unsuspicious, to deal him one terrible swashing blow, and end forever the lawless doings of the Tailless Tyke.

The moon flung off its veil of cloud. White and cold, it stared down into the Devil's Bowl; on murderer and murdered.

With a hand's cast of the avengers of blood humped the black boulder. On the border of its shadow lay a dead sheep; and standing beside the body, his coat all ruffled by the hand of the storm— Owd Bob—Owd Bob o' Kenmuir.

Then the light went in, and darkness covered the land.

It was Owd Bob. There could be no mistaking. In the wide world there was but one Owd Bob o' Kenmuir. The silver moon gleamed down on the dark head and rough gray coat, and lit the white escutcheon on his chest.

And in the darkness James Moore was lying with his face pressed downward that he might not see.

Once he raised himself on his arms; his eyes were shut and face uplifted, like a blind man praying. He passed a weary hand across his brow; his head dropped again; and he moaned and moaned like a man in everlasting pain.

Then the darkness lifted a moment, and he stole a furtive glance, like a murderer's at the gallows-tree, at the scene in front.

It was no dream; clear and cruel in the moonlight the humpbacked boulder; the dead sheep; and that gray figure, beautiful, motionless, damned for all eternity.

The Master turned his face and looked at Andrew, a dumb, pitiful entreaty in his eyes; but in the boy's white, horror-stricken countenance was no comfort. Then his head lolled down again, and the strong man was whimpering.

"He! he! he!" 'Scuse ma laffin', Mr. Moore—he! he! he!"

A little man, all wet and shrunk, sat hunching on a mound above them, rocking his shrivelled form to and fro in the agony of his merriment.

"Ye raskil—he! he! Ye rogue—he! he!" and he shook his fist waggishly at the unconscious gray dog. "I owe ye anither grudge for this—ye've anteecipated me"—and he leant back and shook this way and that in convulsive mirth.

The man below him rose heavily to his feet, and tumbled toward the mocker, his great figure swaying from side to side as though in blind delirium, moaning still as he went. And there was that on his face which no man can mistake. Boy that he was, Andrew knew it.

"Feyther! feyther! do'ee not!" he pleaded, running after his father and laying impotent hands on him.

But the strong man shook him off like a fly, and rolled on, swaying and groaning, with that awful expression plain to see in the moonlight.

In front the little man squatted in the rain, bowed double still; and took no thought to flee.

"Come on, James Moore! Come on!" he laughed, malignant joy in his voice, and something gleamed bright in his right hand, and was hid again. "I've bin waitin' this a weary while noo. Come on!"

Then had there been done something worse than sheep-murder in the dreadful lonesomeness of the Devil's Bowl upon that night; but of a sudden, there sounded the splash of a man's foot falling heavily behind; a hand like a falling tree smote the Master on the shoulder; and a voice roared above the noise of the storm:

"Mr. Moore! Look, man! Look!

The Master tried to shake off that detaining grasp; but it pinned him where he was, immovable.

"Look, I tell yo'!" cried that great voice again.

A hand pushed past him and pointed; and sullenly he turned, ignoring the figure at his side, and looked.

The wind had dropped suddenly as it had risen; the little man on the mound had ceased to chuckle; Andrew's sobs were hushed; and in the background the huddled flock edged closer. The world hung balanced on the pin-point of the moment. Every eye was in the one direction.

With dull, uncomprehending gaze James Moore stared as bidden. There was the gray dog naked in the moonlight, heedless still of any witnesses; there the murdered sheep, lying within and without that distorted shade and there the humpbacked boulder.

He stared into the shadow, and still stared. Then he started as though struck. The shadow of the boulder had moved!

Motionless, with head shot forward and bulging eyes, he gazed.

Ay, ay, ay; he was sure of it—a huge dim outline as of a lion *couchant*, in the very thickest of the blackness.

At that he was seized with such a palsy of trembling that he must have fallen but for the strong arm about his waist.

Clearer every moment grew that crouching figure; till at length they plainly could discern the line of arching loins, the crest, thick as a stallion's, the massive, wagging head. No mistake this time. There he lay in the deepest black, gigantic, revelling in his horrid debauch—the Black Killer!

And they watched him at his feast. Now he burrowed into the spongy flesh; now turned to lap the dark pool which glittered in the moonlight at his side like claret in a silver cup. Now lifting his head, he snapped irritably at the rain-drops, and the moon caught his wicked, rolling eye and the red shreds of flesh dripping from his jaw. And again, raising his great muzzle as if about to howl, he let the delicious nectar trickle down his throat and ravish his palate.

So he went on, all unsuspicious, wisely nodding in slow-mouthed gluttony. And in the stillness, between the claps of wind, they could hear the smacking of his lips.

While all the time the gray dog stood before him, motionless, as though carved in stone.

At last, as the murderer rolled his great head from side to side, he saw that still figure. At the sight he leaped back, dismayed. Then with a deep-mouthed roar that shook the waters of the Tarn he was up and across his victim with fangs bared, his coat standing erect in wet, rigid furrows from topknot to tail.

So the two stood, face to face, with perhaps a yard of rain-pierced air between them.

The wind hushed its sighing to listen. The moon stared down, white and dumb. Away at the back the sheep edged closer. While save for the everlasting thunder of the rain, there was utter stillness.

An age, it seemed, they waited so. Then a voice, clear yet low and far away, like a bugle in a distant city, broke the silence.

"Eh, Wullie!" it said.

There was no anger in the tones, only an incomparable reproach; the sound of the cracking of a man's heart.

At the call the great dog leapt round, snarling in hideous passion. He saw the small, familiar figure, clear-cut against the tumbling sky; and for the only time in his life Red Wull was afraid.

His blood-foe was forgotten; the dead sheep was forgotten; everything was sunk in the agony of that moment. He cowered upon the ground, and a cry like that of a lost soul was wrung from him; it rose on the still night air and floated, wailing, away; and the white waters of the Tarn thrilled in cold pity; out of the lonely hollow; over the desolate Marches; into the night.

On the mound above stood his master. The little man's white hair was bared to the night wind; the rain trickled down his face; and his hands were folded behind his back. He stood there, looking down into the dell below him, as a man may stand at the tomb of his lately buried wife. And there was such an expression on his face as I cannot describe.

"Wullie, Wullie, to me!" he cried at length; and his voice sounded weak and far, like a distant memory.

At that the huge brute came crawling toward him on his belly, whimpering as he came, very pitiful in his distress. He knew his fate as every sheep-dog knows it. That troubled him not. His pain, insufferable, was that this, his friend and father, who had trusted him, should have found him in his sin.

So he crept up to his master's feet; and the little man never moved.

"Wullie—ma Wullie!" he said very gently. "They've aye bin agin me—and noo you! A man's mither—a man's wife—a man's dog! they're all I've iver had; and noo ain o' they three has turned agin me! Indeed I am alone!"

At that the great dog raised himself, and placing his forepaws on his master's chest tenderly, lest he should hurt him who was already hurt past healing, stood towering above him; while the little man laid his two cold hands on the dog's shoulders.

So they stood, looking at one another, like a man and his love.

At M'Adam's word, Owd Bob looked up, and for the first time saw his master.

He seemed in nowise startled, but trotted over to him. There was nothing fearful in his carriage, no haunting blood-guiltiness in the true gray eyes which never told a lie, which never, dog-like, failed to look you in the face. Yet his tail was low, and, as he stopped at his master's feet, he was quivering. For he, too, knew, and was not unmoved.

For weeks he had tracked the Killer; for weeks he had followed him as he crossed Kenmuir, bound on his bloody errands; yet always had lost him on the Marches. Now, at last, he had run him to ground. Yet his heart went out to his enemy in his distress.

"I thowt 't had been yo', lad," the Master whispered, his hand on the dark head at his knee—"I thowt 't had bin yo'!"

Rooted to the ground, the three watched the scene between M'Adam and his Wull.

In the end the Master was whimpering; Andrew crying; and David turned his back.

At length, silent, they moved away.

"Had I—should I go to him?" asked David hoarsely, nodding toward his father.

"Nay, nay, lad," the Master replied. "Yon's not a matter for a mon's friends."

So they marched out of the Devil's Bowl, and left those two alone together.

A little later, as they trampled along, James Moore heard little pattering, staggering footsteps behind.

He stopped, and the other two went on.

"Man," a voice whispered, and a face, white and pitiful, like a mother's pleading for her child, looked into his—"Man, ye'll no tell them a'? I'd no like 'em to ken 'twas ma Wullie. Think an 't had been yer ain dog."

"You may trust me!" the other answered thickly.

The little man stretched out a palsied hand.

"Gie us yer hand on 't. And G–God bless ye, James Moore!"

So these two shook hands in the moonlight, with none to witness it but the God who made them.

And that is why the mystery of the Black Killer is yet unsolved in the Daleland. Many have surmised; besides those three only one other knows—knows now which of those two he saw upon a summer night was the guilty, which the innocent. And Postie Jim tells no man.

Sources

Excerpt from *Beautiful Joe* by Marshall Saunders, 1903.

"Uncle Dick's Rolf" by Georgiana M. Craik from *The Junior Classics*, Volume 8, edited by William Patten, 1912.

"Ulysses and the Dogman" by O. Henry from *Sixes and Sevens*, 1914.

"The Baron's Wonderful Dog" by R. E. Raspe from *The Surprising Adventures of the Renowned Baron Munchausen*, 1811.

"Brown Wolf" by Jack London from *Brown Wolf and Other Jack London Stories*, 1920.

"A Yellow Dog" by Bret Harte from *Barker's Luck and Other Stories*, 1896.

"Bingo" by Ernest Thompson Seton from *Wild Animals I Have Known*, 1900.

"A Dark-Brown Dog" by Stephen Crane from *Men, Women, and Boats*, 1920.

"Memoirs of a Yellow Dog" by O. Henry from *The Four Million*, 1907.

"The She-Wolf" by Saki (H. H. Munro) from *Beast and Super-Beasts*, 1914.

"Tito: The Story of the Coyote That Learned How" by Ernest Thompson Seton from *Lives of the Hunted*, 1901.

"A Fire-fighter's Dog" by Arthur Quiller-Couch from *The Junior Classics*, Volume 8, edited by William Patten, 1912.

"Scrap" by Lucia Chamberlain from *The Junior Classics*, Volume 8, edited by William Patten, 1912.

"Carlo, the Soldiers' Dog" by Rush C. Hawkins from *The Junior Classics*, Volume 8, edited by William Patten, 1912.

Excerpt from *Bruce* by Albert Payson Terhune, 1920.

Excerpt from *Three Men in a Boat (To Say Nothing of the Dog)* by Jerome K. Jerome, 1889.

"Philippa's Fox Hunt" by E. Somerville and Martin Ross from *Some Experiences of an Irish R. M.*, 1899.

Excerpt from *Bob, Son of Battle* by Alfred Ollivant, 1898.